CITYPACK TOP 25
Singapore

VIVIEN LYTTON
ADDITIONAL WRITING BY ROD RITCHIE

If you have any comments
or suggestions for this guide
you can contact the editor at
Citypack@theAA.com

AA Publishing
Find out more about AA Publishing and the wide
range of services the AA provides by visiting our
website at www.theAA.com/travel

How to Use This Book

KEY TO SYMBOLS

🚩 Map reference to the accompanying fold-out map

✉ Address

☎ Telephone number

🕐 Opening/closing times

🍴 Restaurant or café

🚆 Nearest rail station

Ⓜ Nearest MRT station

🚌 Nearest bus route

🚤 Nearest riverboat or ferry stop

♿ Facilities for visitors with disabilities

❓ Other practical information

▷ Further information

ℹ Tourist information

✋ Admission charges: Expensive (over S$6), Moderate (S$3–6), and Inexpensive (S$3 or less).

⭐ Major Sight ★ Minor Sight

👣 Walks 🚍 Excursions

🛍 Shops

🎭 Entertainment and Nightlife

🍴 Restaurants

This guide is divided into four sections

• **Essential Singapore:** an introduction to the city and tips on making the most of your stay.

• **Singapore by Area:** we've broken the city into four areas, and recommended the best sights, shops, entertainment venues, nightlife and restaurants in each one. Suggested walks help you to explore on foot.

• **Where to Stay:** the best hotels, whether you're looking for luxury, budget or something in between.

• **Need to Know:** the info you need to make your trip run smoothly, including getting about by public transport, weather tips, emergency phone numbers and useful websites.

Navigation In the Singapore by Area chapter, we've given each area its own color, which is also used on the locator maps throughout the book and the map on the inside front cover.

Maps The fold-out map accompanying this book is a comprehensive street plan of central Singapore. The grid on this map is the same as the grid on The City area locator map and has upper case grid references. Sights and listings within the East Island and West Island areas have lower case grid references.

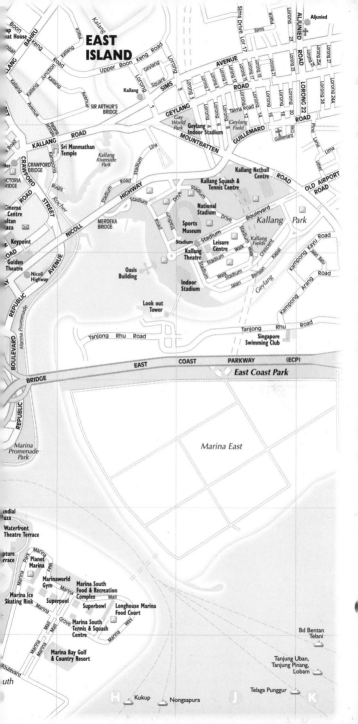

Contents

ESSENTIAL SINGAPORE	4–18
Introducing Singapore	4–5
A Short Stay in Singapore	6–7
Top 25	8–9
Shopping	10–11
Shopping by Theme	12
Singapore by Night	13
Eating Out	14
Restaurants by Cuisine	15
If You Like...	16–18

SINGAPORE BY AREA	19–106
THE CITY	20–48
Area Map	22–23
Sights	24–40
Walk	41
Shopping	42–43
Entertainment and Nightlife	44–45
Restaurants	46–48

WEST ISLAND	49–74
Area Map	50–51
Sights	52–71
Walk	72
Shopping	73
Restaurants	74

EAST ISLAND	75–92
Area Map	76–77
Sights	78–87
Walk	88
Shopping	90
Entertainment and Nightlife	91
Restaurants	92

FARTHER AFIELD	93–106
Area Map	94–95
Sights	96–99
Diving Singapore's Islands	100–101
Excursions	102–103
Walk	104
Shopping	106
Restaurants	106

WHERE TO STAY	107–112
Introduction	108
Budget Hotels	109
Mid-Range Hotels	110–111
Luxury Hotels	112

NEED TO KNOW	113–125
Planning Ahead	114–115
Getting There	116–117
Getting Around	118–119
Essential Facts	120–121
Language	122–123
Timeline	124–125

CONTENTS

Introducing Singapore

The tiny island nation of Singapore is a dramatic fusion of colonial and modern times. A planner's dream, the city has best-practice transportation and communication systems, flashy hotels, glitzy shopping malls, and one of the world's great airports.

Tree-lined avenues, landscaped urban areas, small parks and roadside tropical greenery are commonplace. Singapore's position as a manufacturing and shipping hub, and as one of Asia's premier financial areas, is constantly being strengthened by a government keen to bring new technology and research industries to an island that makes its way forward with human resources as its base. Despite the island's impressive development in the last 50 years, seen in the cityscape of tower blocks, freeways and glitzy shopping areas, pockets of old Singapore remain.

The diversity of races—Chinese, Malay and Indians, joined by workers from Western nations and other parts of Asia—and their many religions and creeds, exemplified by Singapore's many festivals and traditions, make the city a most fascinating and vibrant destination.

Located just over 60 miles (100km) north of the equator, the island's tropical climate, with humidity often above 90 percent, can sap the energies of even the most ardent traveler. Fortunately air-conditioning rules in Singapore —shops, hotels and public transportation are all climate-controlled.

So board a bus, ride the MRT, or hail a cab and explore the delights of this cosmopolitan island state. The near-city neighborhoods each have a distinct character based on their ethnic or colonial origins. Visit some of the backstreets of Chinatown, the temples in Little India, and the markets around the mosques at Ramadan, and you'll experience a different Singapore from the shopping frenzy of Orchard Road.

Facts + Figures

- **Population in 1819: 500; population in 2006: 4.5 million**

- **Religions: Taoist/Buddhist 54%; Muslim 15%; Christian 13%; Hindu 4%; other/none 14%**

SINGLISH

You're bound to come across Singlish, the local colloquial English, if you talk to many Singaporeans. You'll know someone is speaking Singlish if they throw the word *lah* in at every opportunity to show emphasis. Other examples include: *fli-end* (friend), *tok kong* (very good) and *lerf* (love).

SURROUNDING ISLANDS

While the best-known island is the recreational Sentosa (▷ 60), once a British fort, the country is surrounded by over 50 small islands. While they're mostly occupied by the military, oil refineries or nature reserves, St. John's Island (▷ 98) in the south is a popular picnic destination and Kusu Island has a turtle sanctuary.

A FINE CITY

You may have heard that Singapore is a fine city (you can even buy the T-shirt). The government's perfectly reasonable campaign to keep the city clean, and its citizens socially responsible, has led to fines of up to S$1,000 for such acts as littering, jaywalking or even failure to flush a public toilet.

A Short Stay in Singapore

DAY 1

Morning Have an early breakfast and head for the **Botanic Gardens** (▷ 52–53) for a walk among the extensive plant collection. Only a few minutes' bus ride from Orchard Road, this tropical botanical treasure-trove is at its best in the cool of the morning.

Mid-morning Take a bus or taxi back into the city and stroll along **Orchard Road** (▷ 32–33). The morning is less crowded than the afternoon and you can always come back when you've found your way around this mega shopopolis.

Lunch Make your way to **Chinatown** (▷ 26–27) for lunch, after a shower and freshen-up in your hotel. There are many authentic hawker centers here for a quintessential Singapore lunch with the locals.

Afternoon Explore Chinatown's back streets where there are many antique and gift shops—be sure to visit the **Singapore Handicraft Centre** (▷ 43). Wander down South Bridge Road to view Singapore's oldest Hindu Temple—**Sri Mariamman Temple** (▷ 36).

Mid-afternoon Take a bus or taxi to the **Asian Civilisations Museum** (▷ 24–25) and learn about Asian cultures from the excellent displays in this perfectly restored old colonial-period building.

Dinner At **Esplanade** (▷ 28) you'll find a wide range of excellent outdoor dining options by the river.

Evening Head to the **Esplanade Theatres** (▷ 28) for an evening performance—tickets are available from the box office. Wander around the precinct and enjoy the fabulous views of the city at night.

DAY 2

Morning Visit **Raffles Hotel** (▷ 34) at the start of the day, a quieter and more reflective time to wander around one of the world's finest hotels, when you can enjoy a coffee instead of an expensive Singapore Sling. Check out some of the public spaces, including the famed Long Bar and visit the small museum on the second floor. Then head for the nearby **Singapore Art Museum** (▷ 35), housed in a beautifully restored 19th-century school building, which has a fine collection of Southeast Asian art.

Mid-morning Take a bus to Serangoon Road to have a look in the interesting shops that line the narrow footpaths of **Little India** (▷ 30–31).

Lunch Serangoon Road has plenty of Indian dining options, but a really economical and tasty lunch can be had at **Komala Vilas** (▷ 48).

Afternoon There's something for everyone at **VivoCity** (▷ 43) in the new Harbourfront redevelopment that adjoins Sentosa, so take the MRT from Little India to Harbourfront.

Mid-afternoon Catch the MRT from Harbourfront to **Clarke Quay** (▷ 38) via Chinatown. Explore the shops and stalls around Clarke Quay and perhaps take a boat ride on the Singapore River.

Dinner The riverside setting of **Clarke Quay** and **Riverside Point** (▷ 38, 42), illuminated by the city lights, makes a perfect evening meal destination. Expatriates congregate here after a hard day at the office for drinks and to dine. There are any number of fine dining options along the river.

Evening There are some good nightspots here, but try **Lox** (▷ 45) if you like soul, R&B and hip-hop.

ESSENTIAL SINGAPORE TOP 25

▶ ▶ ▶

Asian Civilisations Museum ▷ 24–25 Asian history and culture in two stunning buildings.

Sri Mariamman Temple ▷ 36 Singapore's oldest Hindu temple, now a national monument.

Siong Lim Temple ▷ 84 One of Singapore's largest Buddhist temples.

Singapore Zoo ▷ 68–69 Often hailed as one of the loveliest zoos in the world.

Singapore Science Centre ▷ 66–67 Introduces children to science and technology in an entertaining hands-on style.

Singapore Nature Reserves ▷ 64–65 Escape the city to tropical open spaces.

Singapore Discovery Centre ▷ 62 A fascinating, world-class "edutainment" attraction.

Singapore Art Museum ▷ 35 Local and Asian art is beautifully displayed at this state-of-the-art gallery.

Botanic Gardens ▷ 52–53 Superbly land-scaped gardens full of tropical and subtropical flora.

Sentosa ▷ 60–61 An island playground with a fabulous cable-car ride.

Changi Chapel & Museum ▷ 78 A moving record of conditions endured by prisoners held during WWII.

Republic of Singapore Air Force Museum ▷ 82–83 Get an insight into the history of aviation.

These pages are a quick guide to the Top 25, which are described in more detail later. Here they are listed alphabetically, and the tinted background shows which area they are in.

Chinatown ▷ 26–27
Conveys something of the flavor of old Singapore.

East Coast Park ▷ 80–81
Singaporeans head to this beachside area for land and sea sports or to just chill.

Esplanade–Theatres on the Bay ▷ 28 A fantastic world-class theater and entertainment complex.

Joo Chiat Road ▷ 79 The traditional Singapore way of life can still be seen in this nostalgic area.

Jurong BirdPark ▷ 54–55
Home to over 9,000 birds from all over the world.

Kampung Glam ▷ 29
Historic district named after the glam tree.

Little India ▷ 30–31 The exotic sights, sounds and smells of southern India.

Mandai Orchid Gardens ▷ 56 Stunning displays of orchids, including Singapore's national flower.

Memories at Old Ford Factory ▷ 57 Charts the history of the Japanese occupation of Singapore.

Night Safari ▷ 58–59
Take the tram ride around this park and see creatures in their night-time habitats.

Raffles Hotel and Museum ▷ 34
One of the world's greatest palace-hotels.

Pulau Ubin ▷ 96–97 An offshore island idyll offering a chance to get away from it all.

Orchard Road ▷ 32–33 A tree-lined boulevard offering some of Singapore's best shopping.

◀ ◀ ◀

Shopping

Shopping in Singapore is a very serious activity. Without a doubt, the city is Southeast Asia's shopping capital and shops seem to outnumber its inhabitants.

Singapore's Orchard Road (▷ 32–33) provides a comprehensive shopping experience equal to other world capitals, and is particularly recommended for brand-name fashion goods, electronics and cameras. But the benefit of Singapore shopping to those interested in ethnic arts and crafts or Asian antiques is that the nation state's racial mix of Chinese, Malay and Indian means that all types of goods from these cultures can be found in the specialist shops, especially those in the different ethnic quarters of the city. From the Chinese area you will find porcelain, masks, silk and traditional paintings; from the Malay there's basketware, Ikat cloth, batiks, puppets, sarongs and leatherware; and from the Indian quarter paintings, jewelry, sculptures and pottery.

Not surprisingly, given Singapore's hot and humid weather, every large building has air-conditioning. Major department stores include Tangs, Robinsons and Takashimaya. Be sure to check out Far East Plaza in Scotts Road for younger fashions. For small, inexpensive souvenirs, take the MRT to Bugis. For cameras and electronic equipment try Lucky Plaza and Sim Lim Square, armed with your STB good retailers guide (▷ 11) and the Funan IT Mall on North

SALE TIME

Visitors from late May to mid-July should take advantage of the Great Singapore Sale. There's hardly a store on the island that doesn't participate in this stock-moving exercise, when goods of all descriptions are marked down. Newspapers are full of advertisements, but you'll find street tables outside stores laden with goods on sale. The sale even has its own website with store coupons and cash prizes at www.greatsingaporesale.com.sg.

Singapore's shopping is some of the best in the world—particularly along the famous Orchard Road

Bridge Road. The huge Marina Square, including Millenia Walk, five minutes' walk from Raffles City MRT station, has lots of homeware shops. Chinatown has a mix of souvenir and antique shops, including the very interesting People's Park Complex—still popular with locals—a good example of Singapore retailing circa the 1960s. In the colonial district try the lovely CHIJMES mall and nearby Raffles City for fashion and food. Antique lovers should check out Tanglin Mall and the Paragon Shopping Centre. For an Indian department store experience, try the Mustafa Centre in Serangoon Road which opens 24 hours, every day of the year. While bargaining in the markets and suburban shops is considered part of the Singapore experience, and most electronic stores and jewelers will allow you to haggle a little, brand-name boutiques and department stores throughout Singapore have fixed and clearly marked prices.

As you would expect, retailing is evolving in Singapore. Shopping has become such a lifestyle activity that new destinations such as VivoCity meld entertainment with shopping in architectually stimulating surroundings. In contrast, the Sunday flea markets at Clarke Quay and the incredible Thieves' Market at Sungei Road are a chance to pick up a bargain and to see yet another side of Singapore's retail scene.

CONSUMER PROTECTION

Since Singaporeans and the 6 million annual visitors to the island take shopping seriously, the Singapore government is very keen to promote hassle-free, safe shopping for consumers. To aid and protect shoppers, the Singapore Tourism Board (STB) publishes a shopping guide (available at tourism offices) which lists good retailers—those preferred retailers chosen for their service and reliability—and a list of retailers to avoid. A special hotline number, 1800 736 2000, has been set up to assist tourists who have had bad retail experiences during their stay in Singapore. You can also email feedback@stb.com.sg.

Shopping by Theme

Whether you're looking for a department store, a quirky boutique, or something in between, you'll find it all in Singapore. On this page shops are listed by theme. For a more detailed write-up, see the individual listings in Singapore by Area.

ANTIQUES AND HANDICRAFTS

Antiques of the Orient (▷ 73)
Burmese Fine Arts (▷ 73)
Lavanya Arts (▷ 90)
Lim's Arts & Crafts (▷ 73)
Mata Hari Antiques (▷ 73)
Singapore Handicraft Centre (▷ 43)

BOOKS

Kinokuniya (▷ 33)
Select Books (▷ 73)

DEPARTMENT STORES

Mohamed Mustafa & Samsuddin Co (▷ 42)
Takashimaya (▷ 33)
Tangs (▷ 43)
Yue Hwa Chinese Products Emporium (▷ 43)

EASTERN TRADING GOODS

Aljunied House of Batik (▷ 42)
Batik Emporium (▷ 90)
Holland Road Shopping Centre (▷ 73)
Indian Bazaar (▷ 90)
Malay Village (▷ 90)
Poppy Fabric (▷ 90)
Thandapani Co (▷ 90)

ELECTRICAL AND ELECTRONIC GOODS

Apple Centre at Funan (▷ 42)
Cathay Photo Store (▷ 42)
Funan Centre (▷ 42)
Sim Lim Square (▷ 90)

SHOPPING MALLS AND STREETS

Arab Street (▷ 38)
Bintan Mall (▷ 106)
Bugis Street (▷ 38)
Centrepoint (▷ 42)
Chinatown Point (▷ 42)
Changi Village (▷ 90)
Clarke Quay and Riverside Point (▷ 42, 38)
The Heeren (▷ 42)
Johor Bahru Duty Free Complex (Zon) (▷ 106)
Lucky Plaza (▷ 42)
Millenia Walk (▷ 42)
Ngee Ann City (▷ 33)
Orchard Road (▷ 32–33)
Parco Bugis Junction (▷ 90)
People's Park Complex (▷ 43)
Plaza Pelangi (▷ 106)
Specialists' Shopping Centre (▷ 43)
Suntec City Mall (▷ 43)
Tanglin Mall (▷ 73)
Tanglin Shopping Centre (▷ 73)
Temple/Pagoda/Trengganu Streets (▷ 43)
VivoCity (▷ 43)

WATCHES AND JEWELRY

Apollo Goldsmiths (▷ 90)
Pidemco Centre (▷ 43)
Terese Jade & Minerals (▷ 73)

Singapore by Night

Singapore is one of the world's great night cities, whether you want to shop, party or enjoy a meal.

Stepping Out

Retail stores remain open until 9 or 10pm daily, hawker food stands—with their incomparable aromas wafting through the streets—and restaurants provide fantastic choices of cuisine, and bars and clubs are often still packed into the early hours, particularly on Friday and Saturday nights. Main areas to head for include Orchard Road (especially Emerald Hill); Boat, Robertson and Clarke quays; Chinatown (Far East Square district); and the Colonial District (CHIJMES). Around Bugis Street there's always some action, although the area is not as risqué as it was in times past, when it was the city's transsexual meeting place. If you are looking to mix with expats, try Holland Village or the Orchard Road hotels. Finally, you're generally safe wherever you go, since assaults on tourists are virtually unheard of in Singapore.

Riverside Action

Arguably the best choice for those new to town is to head for Boat Quay or Clarke Quay/Riverside Point (▷ 38, 42) districts. Both areas have pedestrian walkways, lots of bars, clubs and restaurants to choose from, and a riverside nightlife ambiance that is typically Singaporean. Alternatively, take an evening river cruise to get a different perspective of this vibrant city, with its contrasting old and new architecture and the night lights. Or head for one of the city's many nightspots (▷ 44–45) for live or house music and a chance to party with the locals.

There's plenty to do in Singapore at night. It's a safe city, too

---

DRINKING OUT

To get the night off to a good start, and to compensate for Singapore's generally high drink prices, take advantage of the happy hours that run from around 5–8pm. Also, many places offer cheap or free drinks for women—check with bars and clubs beforehand (▷ 44, 45).

Eating Out

From such a vibrant and polyglot society you would expect an equally diverse range of food and restaurant choices, and Singapore does not disappoint.

Whether you want to eat a spicy dish wrapped in a banana leaf in a crowded, noisy food hall, or sit down in air-conditioned grandeur and dine on haute cuisine to the tinkling playing of a baby grand, Singapore offers you both choices and everything in between.

Culinary choices come from Malaysia, China, India and Indonesia, and "Singapore food" is a development of all of these. Cantonese cooking is prevalent, but so are the lesser-known food choices from Southern China, either hawked in the street at steaming food stalls where the occupants talk at rapid-fire speed, or in tiny Chinese restaurants tucked away in Chinatown's back alleys.

Indian food is known the world over, but here you can try Malay Muslim or Indian Muslim fare. Known as "Mamak" food, you will know where to go to get this by looking for the restaurant signs written in Arabic.

For coffee, by all means head for Starbucks, but Singapore's traditional coffee shops are no-nonsense, cheap and cheerful options for popular rice and noodle dishes, along with coffee that is thick and sweet.

HAND OR CUTLERY?

Many Hindus and Muslims eat their food with the right hand only; it is considered unclean to eat with the left hand, although it's okay to use utensils—usually a fork and spoon. Eating with your hand, you tear pieces of chapati (using only one hand) and then soak or scoop up elements of the meal. For rice there's another technique: you add the curries and work up the mixture into balls, which you then pick up and pop—almost flick—into your mouth.

Local cuisine is a fusion of Malaysian, Chinese, Indian and Indonesian

Restaurants by Cuisine

There are restaurants to suit all tastes and budgets in Singapore. On this page they are listed by cuisine. For a more detailed description of each restaurant, see Singapore by Area.

CHINESE

Beng Thin Hoon Kee (▷ 47)
Blue Ginger (▷ 47)
Crystal Jade (▷ 47)
Grand Shanghai (▷ 47)
Imperial Herbal Restaurant (▷ 92)
Lei Garden (▷ 92)
New Hong Kong Restaurant (▷ 106)
Wak Lok Cantonese Restaurant (▷ 92)

INDIAN

Banana Leaf Apollo (▷ 92)
Komala Vilas (▷ 48)
Mango Tree (▷ 92)
Rang Mahal (▷ 48)
Samy's Curry (▷ 74)

OTHER ASIAN FARE

Colours by the Bay (▷ 92)

Hae Bok's Korean Restaurant (▷ 47)
Indochine (▷ 47)
Sinar Bodhi Restaurant (▷ 106)

HAWKER CENTERS

China Square (▷ 47)
Chinatown Complex Food Centre (▷ 47)
East Coast Lagoon Food Centre (▷ 92)
Lau Pa Sat (▷ 48)
Taman Sri Tebrau Hawker Centre (▷ 106)

ITALIAN

Al Forno Trattoria (▷ 74)
Da Paolo e Judie (▷ 47)
La Forketta (▷ 74)
Michelangelo's (▷ 74)
Pasta Brava (▷ 48)
Pete's Place (▷ 48)
Prego (▷ 48)
Rocky's (▷ 74)
Sistina (▷ 74)
Sketches Pasta & Wine Bar

(▷ 92)
Zambucca (▷ 48)

OTHER WESTERN FARE

China Square (▷ 47)
Paulaner Bräuhaus (▷ 48)

SEAFOOD

Chin Wah Heng Seafood (▷ 92)
Jumbo Seafood (▷ 92)
Season 'Live' Seafood (▷ 106)

VEGETARIAN

Komala Vilas (▷ 48)
Original Sin (▷ 74)
Sri Vijaya (▷ 48)
Supernature (▷ 48)

COFFEE AND TEA

Coffee Club, Holland Village (▷ 74)
Raffles Hotel (▷ 34)

If You Like...

However you'd like to spend your time in Singapore, these top suggestions should help you tailor your ideal visit. Each sight or listing has a fuller write-up in Singapore by Area.

SAMPLING LOCAL CUISINE

Sample delicious Asian cuisines at Lau Pa Sat hawker centre (▷ 48), in the business district, where you'll find a wide variety of Asian cuisines at super-low prices.
Indian food that is inexpensive and tasty, and eaten from a banana leaf, can be found at Komala Vilas (▷ 48), in Little India.

OUTDOOR DINING

Head south of Orchard Road to the Singapore River, where Clarke Quay (▷ 38) has many river-side restaurants and bars.
Seafood lovers should head for Jumbo Seafood (▷ 92). There, waterside walking trails will help you lose the pounds you put on over lunch.

Lau Pa Sat (top); crabs at Clarke Quay (above); Orchard Road street sign (below)

ELECTRONIC GOODS

Go to Lucky Plaza (▷ 42), in Orchard Road, to check out several levels of shops selling cameras, iPods and other electricals.
For price comparisons and plenty of stores offering the latest gizmos and electronic wizardry at (almost) fixed prices, head for the Funan Centre (▷ 42).

BRAND-NAME CLOTHES

Start at upmarket Tangs (▷ 43) and Takashimaya (▷ 33), two of Singapore's top department stores.
The huge Ngee Ann City (▷ 33) has eight levels of retail glory.

Designer shop on Orchard Road (right)

LEARNING ABOUT LOCAL CULTURE

Start at the refurbished National Museum of Singapore (▷40) then visit the nearby Asian Civilisations Museum (▷24–25) and the Singapore Art Museum (▷35).

Chinatown (▷26–27) is living culture, so wander around the main streets and back alleys and watch the locals go about their daily chores.

GOING OUT ON THE TOWN

Clarke Quay and Riverside Point (▷42) offer a wide range of drinking, dining and nightclub options. Come here and join the expats in a beer.

Ready to kick back and dance the night away? Then head for Zouk (▷45), Singapore's most famous nightclub.

Singapore Art Museum (top); Clarke Quay (above); Little India (below)

STAYING AT BUDGET HOTELS

The holy grail in this pricey hotel city is good, clean accommodation that won't break the bank. YMCA International House (▷109), in Orchard Road, is an old favorite.

Little India Guest House (▷109), slap bang in the hustle and bustle of Little India, offers basic facilities.

ENTERTAINING THE KIDS

Sentosa (▷60–61) will entertain the young ones for a day or more, with its cable-car ride, beaches and aquarium.

The Singapore Science Centre (▷66–67) has heaps of hands-on interactive exhibits and lots of color and scientific movement.

Singapore Science Centre Human Anatomy section (left)

ESSENTIAL SINGAPORE IF YOU LIKE...

A GIRLS' NIGHT OUT

Singapore night lights (below); Bukit Timah (second top)

The stylish cocktail Post Bar at the Fullerton Hotel (▷ 45) serves a wide selection of classic cocktails in elegant surroundings.
On Thursday night and weekends there are free drinks for women at Lox (▷ 45), where the latest in R&B, hip-hop and soul is played.

A WALK ON THE WILD SIDE

Start early or late to avoid the midday heat for a walk along the trails of Bukit Timah (▷ 64), a patch of primary tropical rainforest within reach of the city center.
Singapore's only protected wetland, the 130ha (321-acre) Sungei Buloh Wetland Reserve (▷ 65), is home to over 500 species of tropical flora and fauna.

CUTTING-EDGE ARCHITECTURE

Nothing in the city is quite as distinctive as the Esplanade Theatre (▷ 28) complex, where you don't need to attend a performance to view the dramatic interior.
Take the elevator to the top of Swissôtel's Stamford (▷ 112), one of the world's tallest hotels, for panoramic views over the CBD.

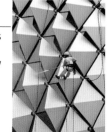

BIRDS AND ANIMALS

Esplanade concert hall roof (above); ostrich at Jurong BirdPark (below)

One of the world's best places to view tropical birds is at Jurong BirdPark (▷ 54–55), where over 8,000 species are kept in aviaries and walk-through enclosures.
Seeing nocturnal animals at a time when they are active is made easy and informative by a ride on the tram at the Night Safari (▷ 58–59).

Singapore by Area

THE CITY

Sights	24–40
Walk	41
Shopping	42–43
Entertainment and Nightlife	44–45
Restaurants	46–48

WEST ISLAND

Sights	52–71
Walk	72
Shopping	73
Restaurants	74

EAST ISLAND

Sights	78–87
Walk	88
Shopping	90
Entertainment and Nightlife	91
Restaurants	92

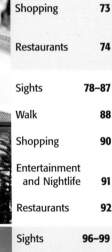

FARTHER AFIELD

Sights	96–99
Diving Singapore's Islands	100–101
Excursions	102–103
Walk	104
Shopping	106
Restaurants	106

Immerse yourself in the galleries of world-class museums, stroll the vibrant streets and back lanes of Chinatown in search of a bargain, or take a walk down Orchard Road for a mind-blowing retail experience.

Sights   24–40

Walk   41

Shopping   42–43

Entertainment
and Nightlife   44–45

Restaurants   46–48

Top 25   **25**

Asian Civilisations Museum
    ▷ **24–25**
Chinatown ▷ **26–27**
Esplanade–Theatres on the
    Bay ▷ **28**
Kampung Glam ▷ **29**
Little India ▷ **30–31**
Orchard Road ▷ **32–33**
Raffles Hotel
and Museum ▷ **34**
Singapore Art Museum ▷ **35**
Sri Mariamman Temple ▷ **36**

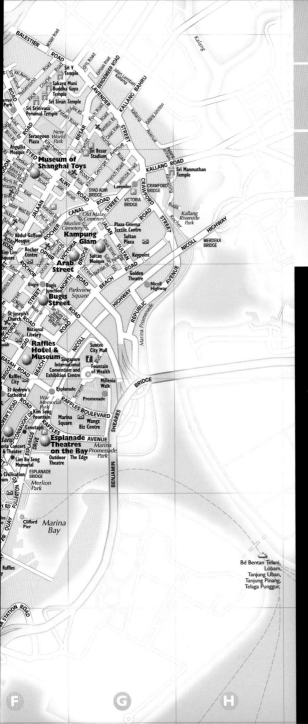

BALESTIER ROAD

Kalang

Sri V
Temple
Sakaya Muni
Buddha Gaya
Temple
Sri Sivan Temple
Sri Srinivasa
Perumal Temple

New
World
Park

Serangoon
Plaza
Angullia
Mosque

Jln Besar
Stadium

**Museum of
Shanghai Toys**

Abdul Gaffoor
Mosque

Rochor
Centre

**Kampung
Glam**

**Arab
Street**

Bugis
Junction

**Bugis
Street**

St Joseph's
Church

National
Library

**Raffles
Hotel &
Museum**

Raffles
City

St Andrew's
Cathedral

War
Memorial
Park
Kim Seng
Fountain

Cenotaph

Marina
Square

ria Concert
& Theatre

Lim Bo Seng
Memorial

**Esplanade
Theatres
on the Bay**

Civilisation
um

Outdoor
Theatre

ESPLANADE
BRIDGE

Merlion
Park

Clifford
Pier

Raffles

SYED ALWI ROAD

LAVENDER STREET

KALLANG BAHRU

BENDEMEER ROAD

KALLANG ROAD

SYAD ALWI
BRIDGE

CANAL ROAD

VICTORIA
BRIDGE

CRAWFORD
BRIDGE

Old Malay
Cemetery
Muslim
Cemetery

Plaza Cinema
Textile Centre

Sultan
Plaza

Sultan
Mosque

Keypoint

Golden
Theatre

KALLANG ROAD

Kallang
Riverside
Park

NICOLL HIGHWAY

MERDEKA
BRIDGE

Nicoll
Highway

NICOLL AVENUE

Parkview
Square

BEACH ROAD

HIGHWAY

REPUBLIC AVENUE

Marina Promenade

Singapore
International
Convention and
Exhibition Centre

Suntec
City Mall

Fountain
of Wealth

Millenia
Walk

Esplanade

Promenade

RAFFLES BOULEVARD

RAFFLES AVENUE

Wangz
Biz Centre

SHEARES BRIDGE

Marina
Promenade
Park

The Edge

BENJAMIN

*Marina
Bay*

Sri V
Temple

Sri Manmathan
Temple

The City

Bd Bentan Telani,
Lobam,
Tanjung Uban,
Tanjung Pinang,
Telaga Punggur,

F   G   H

Asian Civilisations Museum

TOP 25

HIGHLIGHTS

- Chinese history timeline
- *Nonya* porcelain
- Red bat motifs
- Buddhist statues
- Literati gallery
- Jade collection
- Qing Dynasty porcelain
- Kang tables
- Islamic collection

TIP

- Guided tours, given several times a day, are the perfect way to learn more about Asian culture.

Displaying relics of mainland China, continental India, Islamic West Asia and Southeast Asian cultures, this excellent museum is housed in two of Singapore's finest colonial buildings.

Two museum locations In 1997 the beautiful Tao Nan School, which dates from 1910, was opened as the first phase of the Asian Civilisations Museum (ACM I). This museum is currently closed for renovation and will reopen as the world's finest repository of Peranakan culture in 2009. The second phase of the museum (ACM II) is housed in the imposing 1865 Empress Place building. The museum presents a fascinating insight into China, Southeast and West Asia, including the artistic, cultural and historical development. Together with the newly refurbished

Clockwise from left: a sandstone figure of Buddha (Cambodia, 11th–12th century); a Chinese porcelain Buddha; the museum exterior; a Kraak dish showing two Persian ladies of the Safavid period; Lakhoun Khaol dance mask from Cambodia and a gamelan display

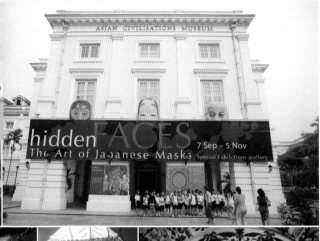

National Museum of Singapore (▷ 40) and the prestigious Singapore Art Museum (▷ 35) these institutions are managed by Singapore's National Heritage Board.

Empress Place This building, with 11 themed galleries spread over three levels, displays over 1,300 artifacts that represent a microcosm of Asian civilizations. The story of Asia is showcased with displays, interactive exhibits and multimedia presentations to help you learn more about the multi-faceted aspects of Asian cultures. The Singapore River Gallery tells many stories, of Chinese 'coolies', indigenous Orang Laut from Malaya and the more recently arrived Europeans. Part of the West Asia gallery has space dedicated to an explanation of the importance of the mosque in Islamic societies.

THE BASICS

www.acm.org.sg
⊞ E5
✉ 39 Armenian Street; 1 Empress Place
☎ 6332 7798
🕐 Mon 1–7, Tue–Sun 9–7, (Fri until 9)
🍴 Empress Place: café, restaurant
🚇 City Hall; Raffles Place
🚌 14, 16, 36, 65, 77, 124, 133, 167, 171, 190
♿ Good
💷 Inexpensive
❓ Free guided tours Mon 2pm, Tue–Fri 11am, 2pm; Sat, Sun 11am, 2pm, 3pm, 4pm. Museum shops. Temporary exhibitions

Chinatown

HIGHLIGHTS

● Maxwell Road hawker center
● Ann Siang Hill
● Chinese shophouses
● Chinese lanterns
● Chinese museum

TIP

● Come prepared for lots of walking as you'll be tempted to check out interesting back-streets.

The best time to visit is just before Chinese New Year, when the streets throb and vibrant stands sell everything from waxed ducks to *hong bao*, red packets for giving money as presents.

Singapore's Chinatown This area covers the streets leading off South Bridge Road between Maxwell Road and the Singapore River. As a policy, conservation of the old buildings goes hand-in-hand with new development here, and though an improvement over destruction, the often rather cosmetic results and years of unsympathetic infill-ing have left only a few streets with the authentic atmosphere and activities of old Chinatown.

What to see Erskine Road and Ann Siang Hill exhibit some of the best efforts of preservation.

Clockwise from left: detail from Thin Hock Keng Temple; outside Thain Hock Keng Temple; aerial view of Chinatown; umbrellas for sale; shop façades and Maxwell Road hawker center

Temple, Pagoda and Trengganu streets have many traditional shophouses and coffee shops. People's Park Complex, on Eu Tong Sen Street, offers a wide range of goods, some very local in character, such as Chinese herbs and good jewelry. East of South Bridge Road, along Lorong Telok and Circular Road, are some examples of nicely decaying shophouses that have yet to feel the hand of the conservationist. Telok Ayer Street, although much renovated, is also worth a visit. Thain Hock Keng Temple (the Temple of Heavenly Happiness) is the oldest and most beautiful Chinese temple in the city. After years of restoration, it now welcomes visitors again. The original temple was built in 1840 by Hokkien immigrants grateful for a safe journey. Far East Square includes Fuk Tak Ch'i, a former temple that now houses a museum dedicated to Singapore's Chinese immigrants.

THE BASICS

✚ E7
✉ South Bridge Road and surrounding streets
🍴 Numerous coffee shops
Ⓜ Chinatown
🚌 2, 5, 12, 33, 51, 61, 62, 63, 81, 84, 103, 104, 124, 143, 145, 147, 166, 174, 181, 190, 197, 520, 851
♿ None
✋ Free

Esplanade—Theatres on the Bay

Esplanade Theatres on the Bay by night (left) and by day (right)

THE BASICS

- ✚ F6
- ✉ 1 Esplanade Drive
- ☎ 6828 8377
- 🕐 Daily 10–10
- 🍴 Cafés, restaurants
- Ⓒ City Hall
- ♿ Good
- ✋ Free entry; tours inexpensive
- ❓ Guided tours (45 mins) in English Mon–Fri 11am, 2pm, Sat, Sun 11am

HIGHLIGHTS

- Twin glass domes
- Waterfront vistas
- High-quality performances
- Stunning concert hall
- Free performances
- Excellent restaurants
- Esplanade Mall shopping

Singapore's stunning new waterfront theater and entertainment complex, dubbed the Durians for its two striking domes, represents the government's serious attempt to attract world-class performers and the best local talent.

Cutting-edge architecture The S$600-million Esplanade is a bid for regional arts excellence. The architect's challenge, given the tropical climate and the desire to present patrons with a dramatic view of the surroundings, was to design an essentially glazed building that was protected from the sun and heat. The fixed exterior triangular aluminum sun shields, set to be opened or closed depending on the angle of the sun, were the final design solution.

World-class facilities The Esplanade includes the Concert Hall, with 1,600 seats and a 200-seat choir stall; the Lyric Theatre, seating 2,000, modeled on a traditional Italian opera house with one stall and three tiers; and a smaller theater for drama, dance and recital, with 750 seats. Internal venues were designed to accommodate the louder and more percussive styles of Asian performances, although the flexible acoustics also suit Western orchestras.

Shopping and dining Esplanade Mall, on three levels, offers a diverse retail mix, from fashion to flowers, home decorations to handmade pottery, and there are several premier restaurants and specialty cafés and bars.

Sultan Mosque (left);
at prayer in the
mosque (middle) and
pashminas on sale
(right)

Kampung Glam

The impressive golden domes and minarets of Sultan Mosque, glinting in the late-afternoon sun, and the call of the muezzin, remind you that this area of Singapore is very much part of the Islamic world.

In the past Kampung Glam, where the Sultan of Singapore lived, was set aside in the early days for Malay, Arab and Bugis traders. The "Glam" may be named after the *gelam* tree from which medicinal oil was produced.

Today Although there are 80 mosques on the island, Sultan Mosque is the focus of worship for Singapore's Muslim (mainly Malay) community. There has been a mosque on this site since 1824, when the East India Company made a grant for its construction. The present mosque dates from 1928, and reveals an interesting mix of Middle Eastern and Moorish influences. Its gilded dome is impressive; unusually, its base is made from bottles. Seen as you walk up Bussorah Street, with its shophouses at the rear, the mosque is truly stunning. Visitors are welcome outside prayer times, as long as they are well covered—no shorts. The *istana* (palace), built in the 1840s, is at the top of Sultan Gate and is well worth a look. The surrounding streets are good sources for *souk* items like basketware, perfume, batik and leather goods. The nearby Muslim coffee shops serve a wide range of Indian Muslim dishes, such as *murtabak* (pancake with various fillings) and *mee goreng* (spicy fried noodles).

THE BASICS

Sultan Mosque
✚ G4
✉ 3 Muscat Street
☎ 6293 4405
🕐 Daily 11–7
🍴 Numerous coffee shops
Ⓜ Bugis
🚌 2, 32, 51, 61, 63, 84, 133, 145, 197
♿ None
🖐 Free

HIGHLIGHTS
● Bussorah Street
● Gilded dome of Sultan Mosque
● Prayer hall
● Istana Kampung Glam
● Murtabak
● Batik

HIGHLIGHTS

- Sari shops
- Banana-leaf meals
- Fish-head curry
- Perfumed garlands
- Fortune-tellers
- Temples
- Spice shops
- Gold merchants

TIP

- The district comes alive with throngs of Singapore's Indian guest workers on Saturday nights.

Along Serangoon Road and the surrounding streets you can snatch all the sensations of India. Exotic aromas fill the air. Baskets overflow with spices. Stores are packed with colorful cloth.

Origins of Little India In the mid-19th century, lime pits and brick kilns were set up in the area, and it is thought that these attracted Singapore's Indians, who were laborers for the most part, to Serangoon Road. The swampy grasslands here were also good for raising cattle, another traditional occupation of the Indian community.

Little India today The district remains overwhelmingly Indian, full of sari-clad and Punjabi-suited women, spice shops, jasmine-garland sellers, Hindu temples and restaurants. Architectural gems

Clockwise from left: garland stall on Serangoon Road; banana leaf curry; browsing the shop stalls; gold shop on Serangoon Road; window shutters with garlands; Sri Veeramakaliamman Temple

abound. Apart from the crowded, lively streets and the tempting food emporiums, there is also the huge Zhujiao food market at the beginning of Serangoon Road; upstairs clothes and luggage are for sale. Across from the market, a little way up Serangoon Road, Komala Vilas restaurant (▷ 48) serves wonderful *dosai* (savory pancakes) and *thali* (mixed curries)—all vegetarian—as well as delicious Indian sweets such as milk *barfi*. Walk along Serangoon Road and you will come to Sri Veeramakaliamman Temple, dedicated to the ferocious goddess Kali. Farther on still is the Sri Srinivasa Perumal Temple, with its magnificent 1979 *gopuram* (ornamental gateway). Take a detour to Race Course Road for a selection of Indian banana-leaf restaurants, notably those offering fish-head curry and a great selection of vegetable curries.

THE BASICS

✚ F4
✉ Serangoon Road
🍴 Many restaurants and cafés
🚇 Bugis
🚌 8, 13, 20, 23, 26, 31, 64, 65, 66, 67, 81, 90, 97, 103, 106, 111, 125, 131, 133, 139, 142, 147, 151, 154, 865
♿ Free

Orchard Road

TOP
25

- Specialist shops
- Exclusive designer shops
- Coffee shops
- Borders bookshop
- Books Kinokuniya
- Takashimaya
- Ngee Ann City

TIP

- Don't be tempted to jaywalk on this long road; look for the underground crossing points.

One of the world's great shopping boulevards, Orchard Road is the retail heart and soul of Singapore. Day or night, a stroll from one end to the other is a pleasure, even if you don't shop.

Room to move Wide sidewalks and plenty of potential coffee stops help make encountering the cosmopolitan charms of Orchard Road a pleasure. And escaping the extreme heat that this equatorial city experiences is as easy as dashing into one of the dozens of air-conditioned shopping malls that line the street. Goods from all parts of the world are on offer, including well-priced electrical items, designer fashions, antiques and gifts. Inexpensive food courts are prevalent and there are any number of good restaurants. For a fine walking tour, start at Centrepoint, near Somerset Station, and

Clockwise from left: Louis Vuitton store; ladies' fashion on display; Heeren Junction; Paragon Shopping Mall; Takashimaya Mall; bookstore on Takashimaya Mall

walk to Tanglin Mall at the western end of the street. On the way, pause near the intersection with Scotts Road to drop in at Borders bookstore, or take in a film at the nearby Lido.

Ngee Ann City The most impressive of Singapore's many shopping malls, this complex is especially popular because of its wide range of supplementary services: banks, restaurants, food courts, post office and supermarket. The stylish, pricey anchor store, Takashimaya, offers departmental shopping at its best, with lovely goods and Singapore's best food hall, where sushi is a top seller. Books Kinokuniya, Southeast Asia's largest bookstore, and the plethora of the top-of-the-line brand-name shops such as Chanel, Cartier and Tiffany, are additional draws. The plaza in front of the building buzzes on weekends.

THE BASICS

✚ E5; D5; C4
Ngee Ann City
✉ Orchard Road
🕐 Daily 10–9.30.
Restaurants on upper floors 10am–11pm
🍴 Restaurants, food courts, supermarket
🚇 Orchard
🚌 7, 14, 16, 65, 106, 111, 123, 167, 605
♿ Good
🆓 Free
❓ Post office, with overseas delivery; customer service center; SISTIC outlet; banks

Raffles Hotel and Museum

Raffles Hotel exterior (left); the famous Singapore Sling (middle) and the courtyard (right)

THE BASICS

www.raffleshotel.com
➕ F5
✉ 1 Beach Road
☎ 6337 1886
🍴 2 cafés, bakery, Chinese restaurant, grill, Tiffin room, deli and "fusion" restaurant
🚇 City Hall
🚌 14, 16, 36, 56, 82, 100, 107, 125, 167
♿ Good
❓ Free museum ⏰ Daily 10–7; shopping arcade

HIGHLIGHTS

● Front façade
● Lobby
● Tiffin Room
● Bar and Billiard Room
● Singapore Sling
● Raffles Museum
● Palm Court
● Long Bar

The renovators may have tried too hard— the Long Bar, for instance, was repositioned to allow for a two-story bar to cater to the hordes of visitors—but Raffles remains one of the world's great luxury hotels.

Legend Say "Raffles" and you conjure up an image of the very epitome of colonial style and service. Established by the Sarkies brothers in 1887, the hotel served the traders and travelers who, after the opening of the Suez Canal in 1869, were visiting the bustling commercial hub of Singapore in growing numbers. Within just a decade of opening, the original 10-room bungalow had been expanded and the two-story wings added. The main building, the front part, was opened in 1899. Over the years the Raffles Hotel has acquired a worldwide reputation for fine service and food, with its charming blend of classical architecture and tropical gardens. The elegant Raffles Courtyard is at the back of the main building.

Past clients Over the years guests have included Somerset Maugham, Elizabeth Taylor, Noël Coward, Michael Jackson and Rudyard Kipling. The Raffles Museum is on the second floor, with Raffles Hotel memorabilia, a must-see for anyone nostalgic about the golden age of travel. The nearby Jubilee Hall presents a multimedia show on the hotel's history four times a day. Some 70 specialist shops adjoin the main building.

The Art Museum exterior (left); some of the items on display (middle and right)

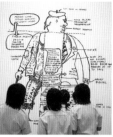

With its focus on art of the 20th century, this is Singapore's flagship art museum dedicated to the collection and display of contemporary works from Singapore and Southeast Asia. It also presents traveling exhibitions.

National treasure The museum, opened in 1996, is housed in the restored 19th-century St. Joseph's Institution building, a former Catholic boys' school, and displays Singapore's national art collection. The permanent collection has grown from under 2,000 artworks to over 6,000, and now houses the largest and most comprehensive collection of 20th-century Southeast Asian art in the region.

State of the art Almost 107,600sq ft (10,000sq m) of floor space includes 14 galleries, a reference library, an auditorium, a multipurpose hall, a museum shop, courtyards and an electronic E-image Gallery that runs interactive programs featuring some of the museum's collection on a large visual monitor. Check out the nearby café that looks out over Queens Street.

On show An overview of Singaporean art is on permanent display and traveling exhibitions expose the region internationally. A community program covers a diversity of art trends and practices, fringe activities and lectures. Check out Georgette Chen's striking *Self Portrait* (1934) and Chong Fah Cheong's tongue-in-cheek *Family and One* (1985).

THE BASICS

www.nhb.gov.sg

F5

71 Bras Basah Road

6332 3222

Daily 10–7 (Fri 10–9)

Café adjacent

Dhoby Ghaut

14, 16, 36, 56, 82, 100, 107, 125, 167

Few

Inexpensive, free admission Fri 6–9

Free guided tours Tue–Fri 11am, 2pm, Sat, Sun 11am, 2pm, 3.30pm. Museum shop

HIGHLIGHTS

- 19th-century building
- Large collection
- E-image Gallery
- Library
- Museum
- Temporary exhibitions

Sri Mariamman Temple

The Temple features many colorful carved deities (left, right and opposite) and is a busy place of worship (middle)

THE BASICS

- ✛ E7
- ✉ 244 South Bridge Road
- ☎ 6223 4064
- 🕐 Daily 7am–9pm
- Ⓜ Chinatown
- 🚌 SBS bus 61, 103, 166, 197 from City Hall MRT
- ♿ None
- 👎 Free

HIGHLIGHTS

- *Gopuram*
- *Thimithi* festival
- Main doors
- Principal hall
- Ceiling frescoes
- Shrines

This is Singapore's oldest Hindu temple, a technicolor shrine with brilliant statuary on the tower over the entrance. It is rather surprising to find it in the middle of Chinatown, but there has long been a Hindu temple here.

Origins The first temple was erected in 1827 by Nariana Pillai, Singapore's first Indian immigrant who became a successful trader and leader of the Hindu community. The original temple, made of wood and *atap* (nipa-palm leaves), was replaced by a brick structure in 1843. This building was later restored and extended. The temple is dedicated to the goddess Mariamman, said to have powers to cure epidemics such as cholera and smallpox.

What to see This temple shows the three principal elements of Dravidian architecture: an interior shrine (*vimanam*) covered by a decorated dome, an assembly hall (*madapam*) used for prayers and an entrance tower (*gopuram*) covered with brightly painted Hindu deities. The splendid *gopuram* was not erected until 1903. The preferred venue of most Hindu weddings, the temple is also the focus for the annual *Thimithi* festival, when devotees walk across a pit of glowing coals—supposedly painless—to honor the Hindu goddess Draupathi. The temple is still very much a place of worship and you must respect this and remember to remove your footwear before entering.

More to See

ARAB STREET

Good handicrafts from all over Asia can be bought near the intersection of Beach Road and Arab Street, where some of the area's original shops still survive. Look for basketware, textiles, lace, silverwork, jewelry and perfume. This is the best area in Singapore for buying fabric; numerous shops offer silks, cottons and batiks.

⊞ G4 ⊠ Area bounded by Jalan Sultan, Beach Road, Ophir Road and Victoria Street ◎ Bugis

BUGIS STREET

Bugis Street was rebuilt in 1991, 449ft (137m) from its original site. Six blocks of Chinese shophouses and some of the more celebrated original buildings were re-created and filled with outdoor cafés and specialty shops. The night market is open until late. Luxury goods, generally fake, tend to be sold near Victoria Street, and you can buy crafts and curios farther down the road, fruit and vegetables near Albert Street.

⊞ F5 ⊠ Bugis Street ◎ Market open daily until midnight. Bars open daily to 2 or 3am ⊞ Open-air restaurants, fast-food outlets ◎ Bugis ⊟ 2, 5, 7, 12, 32, 61, 62, 63, 84, 130, 160, 197, 520, 851, 960 ⊟ Few (pedestrian precinct) ⊞ Moderate bars and food, antiques and crafts

CHETTIAR TEMPLE

The temple of Sri Thandayuthanapani, rebuilt in 1984, is also called Chettiar Temple after the Indian *chettiars* (moneylenders) who financed its construction in the 1850s. The *gopuram* is a riot of images and colors. Each glass panel of the unusual 48-panel ceiling frieze, brought from India, features a deity from the Hindu pantheon.

⊞ E6 ⊠ Tank Road ☎ 6737 9393 ◎ Daily 8–12, 5.30–8.30 ◎ Dhoby Ghaut ⊞ Free

CLARKE QUAY

www.clarkequay.com.sg
Once a riverside area of old wharves and warehouses destined for refurbishment, Clarke Quay, along Singapore River, has been transformed

Arab Street shop display (left)

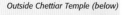

Outside Chettiar Temple (below)

by one of Singapore's most ambitious restoration schemes. The new Clarke Quay opened in 1993 with brand-new godowns, shophouses and trading posts constructed along the riverfront and in the streets leading up to River Valley Road. A vibrant junk that doubles as a restaurant is moored in the river. The entire area is given over to shops and eateries—you can buy everything from pottery and leather goods to wooden clogs, batik prints and Chinese medicines.

✚ E6 ✉ 3 River Valley Road ☎ 6227 8001 🍴 Numerous 🚇 Raffles Place 🚍 SBS bus 54 from Scotts Road; 32, 195 from City Hall MRT ♿ Few ✋ Free

FUK TAK CHI MUSEUM

This was the first Chinese temple in Singapore. The temple originally stood right on the waterfront. Newly arrived Chinese immigrants would hop off their boat after a long hard voyage and go straight into the temple to thank the gods for a safe passage, and to ask for prosperity in business. Thanks to land reclamation, it now stands in the middle of Far East Square on the edge of the financial district.

✚ E7 ✉ Telok Ayer Street ☎ 6227 7531 (Far East Square) 🚇 Raffles Place ✋ Free

MUSEUM OF SHANGHAI TOYS

www.most.com.sg

The world's first museum to exclusively show toys originating from China, the compact museum has three levels of exhibition space. Look out for such delightful and nostalgic exhibits as an electric tram from the 1920s, an Ada Lunn Doll dating from the 1950s, and an ethnic doll from the 1960s. There is a souvenir and retail shop on the ground floor.

✚ F4 ✉ 83 Rowell Road ☎ 6294 7747 🕐 Mon–Sun, 10am–8pm 🚇 Farrer Park ♿ Good ✋ Moderate

NAGORE DURGHA

This undeniably picturesque small mosque, close to Thain Hock Keng Temple, was built around 1820 for the Indian Muslim Community by Chulias, southern Indian Muslims from the

A restaurant kitchen in Clarke Quay (above)

Coromandel Coast. Painted in white and green, it has tiny minarets and a façade of small archways and delicate plaster grilles.

➕ E7 ✉ 140 Telok Ayer Street ☎ 6324 0021 🕐 Daily 10–10 🚇 Raffles Place 🎟 Free

NATIONAL MUSEUM OF SINGAPORE

www.nationalmuseum.sg

The museum building, a fine example of colonial architecture, was opened as a library in 1887. After an extensive renovation, the museum is now a venue for themed exhibitions and displays 11 national treasures, dating from the 14th century to the 1950s. These include the Singapore Stone and William Farquhar's exquisite flora and fauna illustrations. There are also temporary exhibition galleries.

➕ E5 ✉ 93 Stamford Road ☎ 6332 5642 🕐 Daily 10–6 🚇 Dhoby Ghaut 🚌 7, 14, 64, 65, 97, 103, 106, 111, 124, 131, 166, 171, 190 ♿ Good 🎟 Inexpensive

THE PADANG

Once the Padang directly faced the sea, but land reclamation in Marina Bay has long since changed its outlook. The Padang, which goes back to Raffles' days, has retained its use as a recreational area. Cricket and rugby matches are played—in season—and while non-members may not venture into the clubs at either end of the Padang, they can stand and watch the games. City Hall, facing the Padang, has seen several historic events: the herding of Europeans onto the Padang on the morning of the Japanese occupation, and the formal surrender of the Japanese on its steps in 1945. At the southern end is the Cricket Club, with a commanding view of the Padang. The group of government buildings includes the attorney-general's chambers (resembling a small opera house), the Victoria Theatre and Concert Hall buildings, and the former Parliament House.

➕ F6 ✉ St. Andrew's Road 🚇 City Hall 🚌 10, 70, 75, 82, 97, 100, 107, 125, 130, 131, 167, 196 ♿ None 🎟 Free

Padang baseball player (left)

Nagore Durgha shrine (below)

Around Singapore's Historic Core

Get a feel for both the old and new Singapore with this long walk that includes temples and the grand Raffles Hotel.

DISTANCE: 5 miles (8km) **ALLOW:** 5 hours

START

MAXWELL ROAD
✚ E7 🚇 Tanjong Pagar

END

ARAB STREET
✚ G4 🚇 Bugis

① From Maxwell Road walk down South Bridge Road to Smith Street on your left; take this and return to South Bridge Road via Trengganu, Temple and Pagoda streets.

② Note the renovated Chinese shophouses and visit the Sri Mariamman Temple (▷ 36). Cross over and take Ann Siang Hill, then turn left down Club Street.

③ Turn right at Cross Street and left into Telok Ayer Street. Far East Square and China Square are full of places to eat. Check out Fuk Tak Chi Museum (▷ 39).

④ Turn right down Cheang Hong Lim Street and left at the end. Follow Cecil and D'Almeida streets into Raffles Place. Continue into Bonham Street and left into Boat Quay.

⑧ Wander around the streets lined with old shops selling cloth and handicrafts. Head back to your hotel.

⑦ After Raffles City is Raffles Hotel (▷ 34). Continue along Beach Road. Turn left into Arab Street, right into Baghdad Street and left into Bussorah Street. Facing Sultan Mosque, take the side street to your left, then head up Arab Street to Victoria Street.

⑥ Cross over and pass Empress Place and the Victoria Concert Hall and Theatre. On the right is the Singapore Cricket Club. Cross over High Street and take St. Andrew's road. The Padang is on your right.

⑤ Walk along the riverbank until you come to Cavenagh Bridge.

THE CITY

WALK

Shopping

SHOPPING

THE CITY

ALJUNIED HOUSE OF BATIK

One of many good batik shops on Arab Street, Aljunied Brothers also carries ready-made dresses, sarongs, tablecloths, shirts, stuffed toys and the like in batik.

✚ G4 ✉ 91 and 95 Arab Street ☎ 6296 6897 ⏰ Mon–Sat 10–6. Closed Fri 12.30–2 🚇 Bugis

APPLE CENTRE AT FUNAN

Mac fans can now get the full range of Apple products, including the iPod.

✚ F6 ✉ 05–07 Funan IT Mall, 109 North Bridge Road ☎ 6336 9929 ⏰ Daily 10–8 🚇 City Hall

CATHAY PHOTO STORE

Carries a great range of traditional and digital cameras and accessories. Knowledgable staff. You can haggle a bit here.

✚ G6 ✉ 2–215 Marina Square, 6 Raffles Boulevard ☎ 6339 6188 ⏰ Daily 10.30–8, Sun 10.30–7 🚇 City Hall

CENTREPOINT

One of the most user-friendly complexes, with good department stores (Robinson's and Marks & Spencer) and shops selling everything from books to clothes and electrical goods, plus restaurants and a supermarket.

✚ D5 ✉ 176 Orchard Road ☎ 6737 9000 ⏰ Daily 10.30–9.30 🚇 Somerset

CHINATOWN POINT

One of Chinatown's earliest shopping centers, containing a variety of shops and eateries, and specializing in local handicraft and gift shops.

✚ E7 ✉ 133 New Bridge Road ☎ 6534 5767 ⏰ Daily 10–10 🚇 Outram Park

CLARKE QUAY AND RIVERSIDE POINT

This area is gaining a reputation as a bargain haunt with its Sunday flea market and over 80 shops selling everything from curios to designer wear. Adjacent to Clarke Quay is Robertson walk.

✚ E6 ✉ 30 Merchant Road ☎ 6532 3435 🚇 Raffles Place

FUNAN CENTRE

A huge range of computers and accessories, as well as photographic equipment.

✚ F6 ✉ 109 North Bridge Road ☎ 6336 8327 ⏰ Daily 10.30–8.30 🚇 City Hall

---

HONG BAO

You may notice small red packets on sale. These *hong bao*, as they are known, are used for giving gifts of money, particularly for weddings and at Chinese New Year, when it is the custom for unmarried children to receive a red packet. Many employers also choose this time of year to give their red packets—bonuses.

THE HEEREN

Popular among the hip and trendy. Browse the three floors of HMV or sip coffee at Spinelli's outdoor café.

✚ D5 ✉ 260 Orchard Road ☎ 6733 4725 ⏰ Daily 10am–11pm 🚇 Somerset

LUCKY PLAZA

Another huge shopping complex, full of small shops selling all manner of goods. Salespeople may be aggressive, so bargain hard.

✚ D5 ✉ 304 Orchard Road ☎ 6295 5855 ⏰ Daily 24 hours 🚇 Orchard

MILLENIA WALK

Over 190 designer and street-smart fashion stores and specialty shops, such as Raoul, jewelers like the Hour Glass and Cortina E'space, and electrical superstore Harvey Norman.

✚ G6 ✉ 9 Raffles Boulevard ☎ 6883 1122 ⏰ Daily 10–8 🚇 City Hall

MOHAMED MUSTAFA & SAMSUDDIN CO

Three floors of a wide range of goods, including clothing, CDs, jewelry, small appliances, stereos, luggage, clocks and cameras, usually at lower prices. Popular with the locals.

✚ F3 ✉ 01/2/3 Serangoon Plaza, 320 Serangoon Road ☎ 6295 5900 ⏰ 24 hours, 7 days 🚌 66, 67

PEOPLE'S PARK COMPLEX

You can buy all manner of goods at this bustling complex in the heart of Chinatown, including traditional remedies and Asian textiles. There are plenty of clothing and electronic shops, too. This is one of the city's oldest shopping centers.

🚇 E7 ✉ 1 Park Road
☎ 6535 9533 🕐 Daily 10–9.30 🚇 Outram Park

PIDEMCO CENTRE

The Pidemco Centre, home of the Singapore Jewellery Mart, is a good starting point to get an overview of the range and cost of jewelry available here.

🚇 E7 ✉ 95 South Bridge Road 🕐 Mon–Sat 10.30–6
🚇 City Hall

SINGAPORE HANDICRAFT CENTRE

Five floors of shops in the heart of Chinatown, where you can find all manner of curios, including antique snuff bottles, carpets and calligraphic works.

🚇 E7 ✉ Chinatown Point, 133 New Bridge Road
🕐 Daily 10–10
🚇 Outram Park

SPECIALISTS' SHOPPING CENTRE

One of Singapore's older shopping centers, named for the doctors who have offices there. This offers a number of boutiques, as well as the John Little

department store and a SISTIC ticket outlet.

🚇 D5 ✉ 277 Orchard Road
☎ 6737 8222 🕐 Daily 10.30–8.30 🚇 Somerset

SUNTEC CITY MALL

One of Singapore's largest shopping malls, divided into four zones: Galleria, Tropics, Entertainment Centre and Fountain Terrace. Features brand-name stores and specialty shops, including the G2000 flagship store and Mango, and French hypermarket Carrefour.

🚇 G5 ✉ 3 Temasek Boulevard ☎ 6821 3668
🕐 Daily 10–8 🚇 City Hall

TANGS

The third floor of this popular department store has shelf after shelf of electronic items.

🚇 C4 ✉ 320 Orchard Road
☎ 6737 5500 🕐 Mon–Sat 10.30–9.30, Sun 11–8.30
🚇 Orchard

BARGAINING

Many Singapore shopkeepers are happy for you to bargain with them and it can save you a significant percentage, even on fairly small purchases. Don't make your first offer until the seller has reduced the opening price at least once. It is considered a matter of honor that once you have settled on a price, you must go through with the deal. Don't bargain if you see "Fixed price" signs.

TEMPLE/PAGODA/ TRENGGANU STREETS

In the streets between South Bridge Road and New Bridge Road, in the heart of Chinatown, shops and stalls sell a tantalizing range of Chinese goods: herbal remedies, porcelain, exotic fruit and gold jewelry. The rich smell of a Chinese favorite, barbecued pork, pervades the streets.

🚇 E7 ✉ Temple Street, off South Bridge Road
🚇 Outram Park

VIVOCITY

www.vivocity.com.sg
Stunning retail and leisure complex on the waterfront, with department stores and brand-name shops, plus cinemas and a hypermarket.

🚇 B9 ✉ Maritime Square
🕐 Daily 9am–12midnight
🚇 Harbourfront

YUE HWA CHINESE PRODUCTS EMPORIUM

This well laid-out department store in the heart of Chinatown has an extensive array of quality merchandise, from traditional and modern clothes to handicrafts, food and household items.

🚇 E7 ✉ 70 Eu Tong Sen Street ☎ 6538 4222
🕐 Mon–Thu 11–9.30, Fri–Sun 11–10 🚇 Outram Park

Entertainment and Nightlife

BAR NONE

Located in the basement of the Marriot Hotel. Resident bands play rock from the 1970s to the present on high-quality sound systems.

➕ C4 ✉ 320 Orchard Road ☎ 6222 8117 🕓 Mon 7pm–2am, Tue–Fri, Sat 7pm–4am, Sun 7pm–3am 🚇 Orchard

LE BAROQUE

Part bohemian, part sophisticate, exuberant Le Baroque features electrifying live music from local rock icon Douglas Oliveiro and Satellite. This bar, nightspot and restaurant's modern Gothic décor features wrought-iron chandeliers, baroque-style paintings, a Roman column and gold tinged walls, and the washrooms have boudoir appeal.

➕ F5 ✉ 1–07 Fountain Court, Chijmes, 30 Victoria Street ☎ 6339 6696 🕓 Mon–Thu 11am–1am, Fri 11am–1am, Sat 9am–1am, Sun 9am–11pm 🚇 City Hall

BOOM BOOM ROOM

Drag queens and stand-up comedy are the staples at this local institution. Check media for current shows and reserve early.

➕ E8 ✉ 130–132 Amoy Street, Far East Square ☎ 6435 0030 🚇 Tanjong Pagar

CARNEGIE'S

This lively bar, with its emphasis on rock music and occasional bar-top dancing, is favored by locals and expats alike.

➕ E8 ✉ 44–45 Pekin Street, Far East Square ☎ 6534 0850 🕓 Tue–Fri 11am–2am, Sat 5pm–3am, Sun 5pm–midnight 🚇 Raffles Place

CLUB EDEN

A hip crowd gathers in this club, modeled on an underground club in New York, for dancing along to the house DJ's garage and dance music. The bar pours specialty drinks such as Citrus Sins, Adam's Apples and Serpent's Bites. Dress is smart casual.

➕ D6 ✉ 3 Canton Street ☎ 6557 2282 🕓 Daily 6pm–3am 🚌 14, 32, 54

WHAT'S ON

Concerts and theater are very popular, particularly for weekend shows. Details of events, their venues and where to buy tickets can be found in Singapore's daily morning newspaper, the *Straits Times*, and various free publications. Tickets are obtainable from SISTIC and TicketCharge outlets at Centrepoint, Tanglin Mall, Wisma Atria, Great World City, Raffles City Shopping Centre, Takashimaya Store, Funan Centre, Junction 8 and Bugis Junction. Bookings ☎ 6348 5555 and 6296 2929.

THE DUBLINER IRISH PUB

Set in a former colonial mansion, this popular pub, with its plush interior, serves excellent food.

➕ E5 ✉ 165 Penang Road ☎ 6735 2220 🕓 Daily noon–2am 🚇 Dhoby Ghaut

EUROPA MUSIC UNDERGROUND

With its prime Orchard Road location, nightly live bands (except Monday) and smart, young crowd, this place was a hit from day one. Retro music and good dance area.

➕ D5 ✉ 360 Orchard Road ☎ 6235 3301 🕓 Daily 6pm–3am 🚇 Somerset

HARRY'S QUAYSIDE

A riverside location close to the city makes this one of Singapore's most popular places for a drink, and the crowd often spills out onto the sidewalk. Blues on Sunday, jazz Wednesday to Saturday.

➕ E6 ✉ 28 Boat Quay ☎ 6538 3029 🕓 Mon–Thu 11am–midnight, Fri, Sat 11am–3am, Sun 11am–1am 🚌 16, 31, 55

LONG BAR AND BAR & BILLARDS ROOM

The Singapore Sling is usually high on a visitor's list of things to taste in Singapore, and the place to enjoy it is undoubtedly the Bar and Billiards Room and the Long Bar, both in the Raffles Hotel (▷ 34), where the drink was first served.

<F5 icon> F5 <mail icon> Raffles Hotel Arcade <phone icon> 6337 1886 <clock icon> Sun–Thu 11am–1am, Fri, Sat 6pm–2am <train icon> City Hall

LOX

Soul, R&B and hip-hop are the house style at this popular place for the young dance crowd. <E6 icon> E6 <mail icon> Block 3C, River Valley Road, 02–04 Clarke Quay <phone icon> 6334 4942 <clock icon> Daily 7pm–3am <train icon> Clarke Quay

MINISTRY OF SOUND

www.ministryofsound.com.sg Progressive house, funky beats, electro, hip-hop/R&B, disco and soulful house from a multi-million dollar sound system complemented by digital imaging projectors and special effects machines. <E6 icon> E6 <mail icon> Block 3C The Cannery, River Valley Road, Clarke Quay <phone icon> 6333 4168 <ticket icon> S$25 inclusive of 2 house-pour drinks <clock icon> Wed–Sat 9pm–4am

NEXT PAGE PUB

Next door to the more hip Front Page, this trendy shophouse, decked out in the Chinese style, is popular with expats and there's a pool table. <D6 icon> D6 <mail icon> 17 Mohamed Sultan Road <phone icon> 6835 1693 <clock icon> Daily 2pm–3am <bus icon> 32, 54, 195

PALONG LOBBY BAR

Located in the Rendezvous Hotel, you get great cocktails in tranquil surroundings. <E5 icon> E5 <mail icon> 9 Bras Basah Road

<phone icon> 6335 1880 <clock icon> Mon–Thu 3pm–11pm, Fri, Sat 3pm–1am, Sun 3pm–midnight <train icon> Dhoby Ghaut

PAPA JOE'S

This vibrant nightspot, with a great Orchard Road location, is popular with locals and expats alike. Enjoy Tex-Mex food with a Mediterranean twist. The mango margaritas are legendary. Great pizzas. <D5 icon> D5 <mail icon> 180 Orchard Road <phone icon> 6732 6966 <clock icon> Daily 5pm–3am <train icon> Somerset

PAULANER BRAHAUS

Offers authentic Bavarian cuisine and the popular, freshly brewed Munich

ONE FOR THE ROAD

After working a 10- to 12-hour day, your average Singaporean either heads home to relax with family members, or, if they are young and single, stops at a favorite bar for a drink en route. Weekends see increased nightlife activity; clubs do a roaring trade and attract expats and locals alike, especially those in the courting mode. As in other large cities, there is a good selection of Irish pubs and October brings a quota of German-inspired beer fests. And don't leave Singapore without having a gin sling at the famous Long Bar at Raffles Hotel (▷ 34).

beer in a range of types. The rustic setting is reminiscent of German microbreweries. <F6 icon> F6 <mail icon> 9 Raffles Boulevard <phone icon> 6883 2572 <clock icon> Sun–Thu 11.30am–1am, Fri, Sat 11.30am–2am <bus icon> 32, 54, 195 <train icon> City Hall

POST BAR

Part of the stylish Fullerton hotel (▷ 112), this bar serves a selection of classic and fruity cocktails. <F6 icon> F6 <mail icon> 1 Fullerton Square <phone icon> 6877 8135 <clock icon> Mon–Fri noon–2am, Sat, Sun 5pm–2am <train icon> Raffles Place

VICTORIA THEATRE AND CONCERT HALL

Classical and other concerts take place here. Check local media for concert and peformance details. <E5 icon> E5 <mail icon> 11 Empress Place <phone icon> 6338 1230 <train icon> Raffles Place

ZOUK

Founded in 1990, this is Singapore's most famous club—with good reason. Excellent in-house and guest DJs spin the discs nightly. It's in a converted godown near the River View Hotel, next to two other good clubs, Phuture and Velvet Underground, all three expensive. <D6 icon> D6 <mail icon> 17–21 Jiak Kim Street <phone icon> 6738 2988 <clock icon> Daily 7pm–3am <bus icon> 16

Restaurants

PRICES

Prices are approximate, based on a 3-course meal for one person.

$$$ over S$50
$$ S$20–S$50
$ under S$20

BENG THIN HOON KEE ($$)

Hokkien food is popular in Singapore, for the ancestors of many Singaporeans lived in southern China, where the cuisine originated. Try duck in lotus leaves.
✚ F7 ✉ 05–02 OCBC Building, 65 Chulia Street ☎ 6533 7708 ⓒ Daily 11–12.45, 6–9.45 Ⓠ Raffles Place

BLUE GINGER ($$)

Set in an old shophouse, this is the best place in Singapore to try Peranakan dishes such as fried port and prawn rolls, *ayam panggang* (chicken in coconut milk) and durian desserts.
✚ E8 ✉ 97 Tanjong Pagar Road, Chinatown ☎ 6222 3928 ⓒ Daily 11.30–2.30, 6–10 Ⓠ Tanjong Pagar

CHINA SQUARE ($)

This sprawling three-floor food complex has Western food outlets and traditional hawker fare under one roof.
✚ E7 ✉ Telok Ayer Street ⓒ Daily 7am–10pm Ⓠ Tanjong Pagar

CHINATOWN COMPLEX FOOD CENTRE ($)

Large buzzing food court in the middle of Chinatown with most types of local Chinese food available plus a range of desserts—try the ice *kacang*.
✚ E7 ✉ Chinatown Complex, Smith Street ⓒ Early until late, daily Ⓠ Chinatown

CRYSTAL JADE ($$)

Traditional Cantonese cuisine including fresh seafood dishes, barbe-cued pork and soups. A real Singapore dining experience.
✚ C4 ✉ 27 Ngee Ann City, 391 Orchard Road ☎ 6238 1661 ⓒ Daily 11.30–2.30, 6.30–10.30 Ⓠ Orchard

SATAY

No trip to Singapore would be complete without the famous satay, a Malay dish. Sticks of chicken, lamb or beef, and sometimes other foods such as tofu, are bar-becued and served with a thick, sweet peanut sauce. Small rice cakes and cucum-ber usually accompany the satay. It is served in some restaurants, and at many hawker centers there is a "satay man." If you develop a taste for it, look in super-markets for the ready-made satay sauce and try it at home with a barbecue.

DA PAOLO E JUDIE ($$$)

People go here for the classic contemporary design, attentive service and modern Italian cuisine. Seafood dishes are the specialty. There's also a bar with plenty of choice.
✚ E7 ✉ 81 Neil Road, Chinatown ☎ 6225 8306 ⓒ Mon–Sat 11.30–3, 6.30–11.30 Ⓠ Outram Park

GRAND SHANGHAI ($$$)

Experience the feel of 1930s Shanghai, with classy décor and a jazz singer. The menu includes soups, noodles and dim sums, smoked eel and roast duck.
✚ C4 ✉ 01–01 Kings Centre, 390 Havelock Road ☎ 6838 6866 ⓒ Daily 12–2.30pm, 7pm–11pm Ⓠ Orchard

HAE BOK'S KOREAN RESTAURANT ($$)

Reliably good Korean dishes such as fried octo-pus with Korean spicy sauce and fried, egg-coated vegetables.
✚ E8 ✉ 44–46 Tanjong Pagar Road ☎ 6223 9003 ⓒ Daily 11.30–3, 5.30–10.30 Ⓠ Tanjong Pagar

INDOCHINE ($$)

This trendy renovated shophouse is a popular drinking spot for expats on weekdays. Vietnamese /Cambodian/Laotian dishes include spicy sausage and fried fish

⊞ E7 ✉ 47c Club Street
☎ 6323 1043 🕐 Daily 12–3,
6–10.30 🚇 Chinatown

KOMALA VILAS ($)

Southern Indian fare is
served here on banana
leaves. It's good and inexpensive, and you can
have unlimited helpings
of the vegetarian food.
For a different drink,
try the sweet, spicy
masala tea.
⊞ F4 ✉ 76–78 Serangoon
Road ☎ 6993 6980 🕐 Daily
7am–10.30pm 🚇 Bugis

LAU PA SAT ($)

This ornate iron building,
built in 1894, is the
largest Victorian filigree
cast-iron structure left in
Southeast Asia. It houses
many of Singapore's best
hawker stalls.
⊞ F7 ✉ 18 Raffles Quay
🕐 24 hours 🚇 Raffles

PASTA BRAVA ($$)

A lovely Italian restaurant
in a converted shophouse
on the edge of
Chinatown. Some dishes
can be expensive, but the
food is very good. This
place is popular with
workers at lunch.
⊞ E8 ✉ 11 Craig Road
☎ 6227 7550 🕐 Daily
11–2.30, 6.30–10.30
🚇 Tanjong Pagar

PAULANER BRÄUHAUS ($$)

German theme restau-
rant-cum-brewery serving
generous platters of
sauerkraut and *wurst
kartoffeln*.

⊞ F6 ✉ 01–01 Millennia
Walk, 9 Raffles Boulevard
☎ 6883 2572 🕐 Daily
11.30–2.30, 6–10 (drinks only
after 10) 🚇 City Hall

PETE'S PLACE ($$$)

This basement trattoria
opened in 1973 and is
popular with both visitors
and locals. The pastas are
tasty and an excellent
salad bar makes the
place a good bet for
vegetarians.
⊞ C4 ✉ Basement, Grand
Hyatt Hotel, 10–12 Scotts Road
☎ 6730 7113 🕐 Daily
1.30–2.30, 6–11 🚇 Orchard

PREGO ($$)

This long-established
restaurant bustles at
lunch and in the evenings
thanks to an excellent
range of dishes and a
perfect central location.
⊞ F6 ✉ Westin Stamford
Hotel, 2 Stamford Road
☎ 6431 5156 🕐 Daily
11.30–2.30, 6.30–10.30 🚇 City
Hall

POPIAH

Popiah—freshly prepared
rice-flour pancakes filled with
a mouthwatering mixture of
onion, turnip, bean sprouts,
minced pork and prawns, all
held together with a sweet
soy sauce and flavored with
coriander, garlic and chili—
makes a delicious snack. You
can order *popiah* in some
restaurants, and many
hawker centers have a
popiah stall.

RANG MAHAL ($$$)

This restaurant has
moved to the ultra-
modern Pan Pacific Hotel
but is still serving a good
range of North Indian
dishes and an extensive
lunch and dinner buffet.
Indian dancers perform.
⊞ G6 ✉ 03–00 Pan Pacific
Hotel, Raffles Boulevard
☎ 6333 1788 🕐 Daily
12–2.30, 7–11 🚇 City Hall

SRI VIJAYA ($)

Modest vegetarian,
banana-leaf establish-
ment offering great value
with its generous helpings
of rice and vegetable
accompaniments.
⊞ F4 ✉ 229 Selegie Road
☎ 6336 1748 🕐 Daily
7am–10pm 🚇 Bugis

SUPERNATURE ($)

Soy burgers, healthy
sandwiches and fresh
juices are the staples at
this chic organic shop.
Vegans well catered for.
⊞ C5 ✉ 01–21 Park House,
21 Orchard Boulevard
☎ 6735 4338 🕐 Mon–Sat
10–8 🚇 Orchard

ZAMBUCCA ($$$)

Italian favorite with retro
décor and lighting. House
specialties include baked
black cod and prawns,
and foie gras with apple
compote and port wine
jus.
⊞ G6 ✉ Pan Pacific 3–7
Raffles Boulevard
☎ 6337 8086 🕐 Daily
11.30am–2.30pm, 6pm–11pm
🚇 Marina Bay

Head west for the world's best bird park, a patch of the island's original tropical rainforest, and hedonistic Sentosa, fast becoming the recreational hub of this dynamic island nation.

Sights	52–71
Walk	72
Shopping	73
Restaurants	74

Top 25

Botanic Gardens ▷ 52–53
Jurong BirdPark ▷ 54–55
Mandai Orchid Gardens ▷ 56
Memories at Old Ford Factory ▷ 57
Night Safari ▷ 58–59
Sentosa ▷ 60–61
Singapore Discovery Centre ▷ 62
Singapore Nature Reserves ▷ 64–65
Singapore Science Centre ▷ 66–67
Singapore Zoo ▷ 68–69

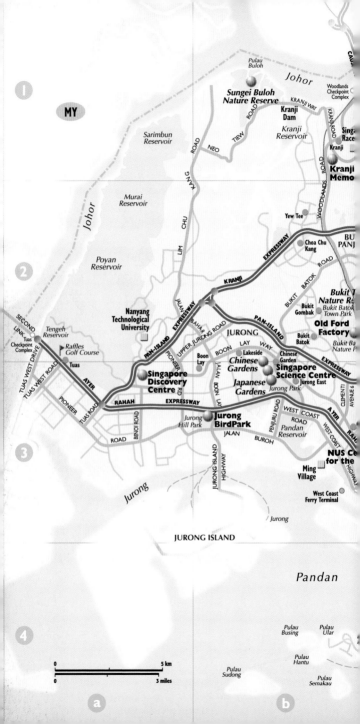

MY

SEMBAWANG

Sembawan
Beach

MIRALTY ROAD WEST

AVENUE 7

CANBERRA LINK

Pulau
Seletar

Johor

ING WOODLANDS

Sembawang

Admiralty

Pulau
Punggol Barat

Woodlands

 ODLANDS

WOODLANDS AVENUE

AI

ROAD

Yishun

Pulau
Punggol Timor

YISHUN

MANDAI

SEMBAWANG AVE

Khatib

Yishun
Park

Mandai
id
ns

MANDAI
ROAD

EXPRESSWAY

Lower Seletar
Reservoir

**Singapore
Zoo**

ht
ari

Upper Seletor
Reservoir

UPPER

Central Catchment
Nature Reserve

THOMPSON

ROAD

Upper Pierce
Reservoir

MacRitchie Trail

**MacRitchie
Reservoir**

PAN-ISLAND

ROAD

LORNIE

Bukit
Brown

**TOA
PAYOH**

DUNEARN

EXPRESSWAY

KIT
IMAH
RD

BUKIT
MAH
ATION

TIMAH

ROAD

Adam

ROAD

**Botanic
Gardens**

Farrer

ROAD

**Colonial
Residences**

HOLLAND

ona
sta

Holland

Commonwealth

NAPIER RD

ORCHARD ROAD

ONWEALTH

AVENUE

One-
North

ALEXANDRA

ROAD

SSWAY

Queenstown

Redhill

JALAN BUKIT MERAH

**Tiong
Bahru**

**Haw Par
Villa**

Telok Blangah
Hill Park

115

COAST

HIGHWAY

Mount Faber

Pasir
anjang

Alexandra

Telok Blangah

Harbourfront

**Harbourfront
Centre**

GATEWAY
AVENUE

Pulau
Brani

Sentosa

Pulau
Tekukor

Pulau
Seringat

Pulau Tembakul
Kusu

Pulau
Jong

Pulau Sakijang Bendera
St Johns Island

Pulau
Darat

Pulau
Subar Laut

Pulau Sakijang Pelepah
Lazarus

u
ng

Pulau
Sebarok

c

d

Botanic Gardens

HIGHLIGHTS

- Rubber trees
- National Orchid Garden
- Jungle Walk
- Palm Valley
- *Myristica fragans*
  (nutmeg tree)
- *Cinnamomum zeylanicum*
  (cinnamon tree)
- Topiary
- Bamboos
- Herbarium

TIP

- Check local papers for
details of the free concerts
that are held in the Garden's
Amphitheater.

**Don't leave Singapore without a visit to
this 128-acre (52ha) botanical wonder,
with its splendid National Orchid Garden.
It is best explored in the relative cool of
the morning or the evening.**

Botanical beginnings Singapore's tranquil botanic
gardens are only a few kilometers from frenetic
Orchard Road. Raffles established botanical gardens at the base of Government Hill in 1822, and
the collection was moved to its present site in
1859. Over the decades, the gardens have been
enlarged and landscaped. The region's first rubber
trees, native to Brazil, were propagated here in
1877, and their descendants are still found in the
gardens. In the 1960s, the gardens supplied many
of the seedlings for roadsides and parks all over
the island, and the greening of Singapore began.

Clockwise from left: the National Orchid Garden; close-up from the National Orchid Garden; the Ginger Garden; the National Orchid Garden; the entrance gate and the Evolution Garden

Highlights The National Orchid Garden has the largest display of tropical orchids in the world—over 1,000 species and 2,000 hybrids—with a Cool House for high-altitude orchids and gardens with orchids in natural settings. On the rolling lawn of Palm Valley you'll find 'islands' of various palms—over 115 genera of the major plant group. The nearby patch of tropical rainforest is one of the few remaining areas of Singapore's original vegetation. Australian Black swans and many other water birds live around the Eco-Lake, where there are displays of herbs and spices, medicinal plants, fruit and nut trees, and bamboos. The visitor center has plant displays, water cascades, a café and a great selection of nature books in its excellent shop. The gardens are popular with locals, who jog, picnic and attend the frequent open-air concerts in Palm Valley.

THE BASICS

www.nparks.gov.sg

✚ c3, A4

✉ Junction of Cluny and Holland roads

☎ 6471 7361

🕐 Daily 5am–midnight; National Orchid Garden daily 8.30am–7pm

🍴 Visitor center restaurant and café

Ⓜ MRT to Orchard, then SBS bus 7, 106, 123 or 174

🚌 As above, plus 75, 105

♿ Good

💷 Botanic Gardens free; admission to Orchid Garden inexpensive

WEST ISLAND ★ **TOP 25**

HIGHLIGHTS

- Penguin feeding time
- Jungle Jewels
- Pelican Cove
- Monorail trip
- Waterfall Aviary
- World of Darkness
- Crowned pigeons
- Birds of paradise
- Southeast Asian hornbills
and South American toucans

TIP

● While the monorail may look a bit of a tourist attraction, it does provide a good overview of the Park.

Hundreds of penguins and puffins crowded together on an icy beach is an unexpected sight near the equator. And don't miss the Waterfall Aviary, where tropical bird species fly almost free.

The world's birds Jurong BirdPark is Asia-Pacific's biggest bird park—49 acres (20ha)—and home to more than 9,000 birds, many from the tropics. Some 600 species, from all over the world, are housed in aviaries and other apparently open enclosures.

Birds of a feather Not far from the entrance, penguins live in a simulated Antarctic habitat with a swimming area. The vast glass-sided tank has windows 98ft (30m) long. The Waterfall Aviary is the most spectacular area, with 5 acres (2ha) of

Clockwise from left: the Lory Loft; flamingoes in the water; the Birds 'n' Buddies show; feeding time; a parrot and the park monorail

forest contained beneath high netting, with more than 1,500 African birds. The aviary also has a 98ft (30m) man-made waterfall. A monorail gives a good overview of the park, but it's well worth getting off to see the birds close up. The South-east Asian Birds Aviary re-creates a rainforest, complete with midday storm, and contains more than 260 species, including the colorful parrots. The African Wetlands exhibit, complete with native-style pavilions, includes the Shoebill and African Crown Crane. Jungle Jewels is a large walk-through aviary devoted to hummingbirds and other South American species. The birds of prey and parrots shows are also entertaining. Twice a day the Birds 'n' Buddies show features comedy, audience interaction and entertaining antics from the park's birds. When you have finished watching birds, cross the road and take a look at the reptile park.

THE BASICS

www.birdpark.com.sg

✚ b3, A7

✉ 2 Jurong Hill

☎ 6265 0022

🕐 Daily 9–6

🍴 McDonald's, Waterfall Kiosk, PFS Terrace Kiosk

🚇 MRT to Boon Lay then SBS bus 194 or 251

♿ Good

💰 Moderate

❓ Bird shows: Birds 'n' Buddies (11am, 3pm), Birds of Prey (10am, 4pm), Children's Parrot Show (1pm)

Mandai Orchid Gardens

The Vanda "Miss Joachim" is the national flower of Singapore (left); the gardens (right)

THE BASICS

www.mandai.com.sg
🕂 c2
✉ Mandai Lake Road
☎ 6269 1036
🕐 Daily 8–7
🚇 MRT to Ang Mo Kio then SBS bus 138
🚌 SBS bus 171 to Mandai Road, then cross road for 138, or TIBS 927
♿ None
💷 Inexpensive
❓ Boxed orchids can be sent abroad—details in shop

HIGHLIGHTS

- Early morning fragrance
- Black orchid
- Tiger orchid
- *Oncidium* "Golden Shower"
- Torch ginger
- Jade vine

Many of the orchid hybrids on display at these gardens are stunning, especially the *Vanda* "Mandai Glow", with its beautiful blend of peach and pale orange.

Cultivation Orchids have been grown on this site since 1951, when the land was leased by a couple of enthusiasts, John Laycock and Lee Kim Hong. It wasn't until 1956 that the gardens were turned into a commercial venture. Following Laycock's death, Amy Ede, his adopted daughter, managed the gardens. The area under cultivation has increased over the years to 10 acres (4ha) and today the orchid gardens are the largest on the island. Millions of sprays are exported all over the world each year, kept in good condition using a unique technology developed by the owners.

The orchids The gardens are packed with gorgeous blooms, some native, some introduced, as well as the many hybrids that have been the making of the Singapore orchid industry. Amazingly, despite the vast array of species on display, all orchids have the same shape—three sepals and three petals, but one of the petals, known as the "lip", is a different shape from the others.

National flower The deep pink and white flowers of *Vanda* "Miss Joaquim", Singapore's national flower, can be seen in abundance, as can many other varieties, including delicate slipper orchids and fantastic moth orchids. An hour's stroll in the gardens, which also contain a landscaped water garden, makes a gentle start to the day.

Inside the museum (left) and a sculpture in the gardens (right)

Memories at Old Ford Factory

It was at this building, on 15 February 1942, Lt.-Gen. A. E. Percival, Commander of the British Forces in Singapore, surrendered to the Japanese Army.

Syonan Years Soon after, Singapore was renamed Syonan-To (Light of the South) and for nearly four years the Japanese ruled Singapore. The art deco style building is now refurbished as a gallery showing the exhibition "Syonan Years: Singapore Under Japanese Rule, 1942–1945".

Hard times The exhibition provides the background of World War II in Malaya and describes the hardships people endured during the Occupation. The pathway leading to the building was the ceremonial route taken by the British forces on the day of the surrender, and you enter the exhibition gallery through a tunnel, starting at the historic Board Room, where the signing of the surrender took place. On display are archival photographs, oral history interviews, maps and artefacts from the era.

"He Ping"–Peace On the mezzanine floor is an AV theatre showing documentaries on various aspects of the Japanese Occupation. In the grounds of the museum is a granite stone inscribed with a Tang dynasty verse entitled "Taking History as a Lesson" and a calligraphic sculpture entitled "He Ping" or Peace, which signifies the relief and calm that comes at the end of war. Behind the old main wing is a garden plot with wartime crops, such as sugarcane and oil palm.

THE BASICS

🔷 b2
✉ 351 Upper Bukit Timah Road Singapore
☎ 6332 7973
🕐 Mon–Fri, 9–5.30; Sat, 9–1.30. Closed on Sun and public holidays
Ⓜ MRT to Clementi then SBS 184
🚌 SBS Bus 170
♿ Reasonable
🍴 Inexpensive

HIGHLIGHTS

● The Board Room
● Wartime crops
● Calligraphic sculpture

Night Safari

HIGHLIGHTS

- "Open" enclosures
- Leopard Trail
- Mouse deer
- Tapirs
- Giraffes
- Lions
- Tigers
- Hippos
- Elephants
- Bats
- Walking trails

TIP

● Check the weather forecast before venturing here, since rain spoils the experience somewhat.

Singapore's Night Safari—a zoo that allows you to see nocturnal animals—is the largest attraction of its kind in the world. Special lights that simulate moonlight illuminate this night zoo.

A world of animals The night safari is divided into eight "geographical" zones that are home to the park's 135 species—more than 900 animals in all. You can expect to see animals from the Southeast Asian rainforests, the African savanna, the Nepalese river valley, the South American pampas and the jungles of Myanmar (Burma). As in the Singapore Zoo, the enclosures are "open" and animals are confined by hidden walls and ditches. Five of these zones have dedicated walking tracks; the others must be visited by tram.

Clockwise from left: close up with the tapirs; the tram is the best way to see the animals; a baby anteater and Chawang, the Asian elephant

Welcome to the jungle The best way to see the Night Safari is to take the tram journey—the tram is silent to avoid frightening the animals. A guide offers commentary as you pass through. Get off at the tram stations and follow the marked walking trails through each zone. You can rejoin the tram anytime; all follow the same route. Avoid using a flash on your camera as it disturbs the animals and fellow visitors.

What to see Listen for the intermittent roaring of the big cats. The Leopard Trail is one of the busiest walking trails. You can see straight into the enclosure of the prowling leopards—only a plate-glass wall separates you from them. On the Mangrove Walk, fruit bats hang overhead in the gloom, and the elephants, giraffes, tigers and lions are always popular.

THE BASICS

www.nightsafari.com.sg
➕ c2
✉ Mandai Lake Road
☎ 6269 3411
🕐 Daily 6pm–midnight
🍴 Restaurant
🚇 Ang Mo Kio MRT, then bus 138 or Choa Chu Kang MRT, then bus 927
♿ Reasonable
💰 Expensive

Sentosa

IMAGES OF

HIGHLIGHTS

● Cable-car ride
● Underwater World
● Images of Singapore
● Butterfly Park
● Fantasy Island
● VolcanoLand
● Cinemania

TIP

● Forget the Sentosa of old, this place is really coming into its own as a recreation, retail, dining and shopping destination.

Even in clean and tidy Singapore the perfect order of Sentosa Island is incredible. The wholesome family package of attractions here is perfect for a fun day with the kids.

Getting there A former pirate lair and British military base, this island playground now attracts more than 4 million visitors a year. Sentosa can be reached across a causeway or by a cable car that runs just over 1 mile (1.5km) from the 380ft (116m) high Mt. Faber. The station is at Harbourfront.

For the active Rent a canoe or windsurfer, follow the well-signed walks and bicycle routes or relax on its 2 miles (3km) of beautiful beaches.

Adventure Watch a volcano erupt every half-hour in VolcanoLand and visit Lost Civilizations, Asian Village or Fantasy Island, which offers 13 water rides and 32 water slides. See more than 350 tropical marine species at Underwater World (feeding times are 11.30, 2.30, 4.30), insects galore at Insect Kingdom and more than 2,500 types of Lepidoptera in Butterfly Park. Audiovisuals and waxworks relate the nation's history in Images of Singapore. Sentosa's Maritime Museum is agreeably low-tech. Visit in the evening for the laser and fountain shows, and check out the spotlighted Enchanted Grove gnome garden. Enjoy panoramic views of Singapore and surrounds from the Carlsberg Sky Tower. Views vary on the revolving seven-minute ride which takes you to a height of 430ft (131m) above sea level.

THE BASICS

www.sentosa.com

➕ c4, A9

✉ Sentosa Island

☎ Sentosa Information Centre 6275 0388

🕐 Mon–Thu 7am–11pm, Fri–Sun, public holidays 7.30am–midnight

🍴 Cafés and restaurants

🚡 Cable car from World Trade Centre (WTC) and Mount Faber

🚇 Harbourfront, then take Sentosa bus

♿ Few

💰 Moderate

Singapore Discovery Centre

The Build It Kids Zone (left); the gateway (middle); the entrance (right) and Little George, the Centre's mascot (opposite)

TOP 25

THE BASICS

www.sdc.com.sg
+ a3, A7
✉ 510 Upper Jurong Road
☎ 6792 6188
🕐 Tue–Sun 9–6 ; Sat 9–8;
closed Mon, except public
and school holidays
🍴 Restaurant and pizzeria
🚇 MRT Boon Lay, then
bus: 193 & 182 from Boon
Lay Bus Interchange
♿ Good
💵 Moderate

HIGHLIGHTS

● Visionarium
● Security Pavilion
● Interactive games
● iWERKS Theatre

WEST ISLAND TOP 25

The Discovery Centre is a world-class "edutainment" attraction that features Singapore's many milestones and achievements in five main galleries.

Visionarium The innovative high-tech exhibits, constructed around eight different themes, present a macro view of the Singapore Story and take you through Singapore's past, present and future, with brilliant light and sound shows and hands-on building activities. One of the highlights is the world's first and largest interactive team-based city design studio, the Visionarium, with a 360-degree screen. During each session, up to 120 guests can design a new city of Singapore and the result is displayed on the huge wraparound screen. A Security Pavilion, with a Crisis Simulation theater, simulates a bomb explosion at an MRT station.

Interactive games The Centre also has several entertaining interactive games and a lively quiz trivia show, located at the Unity Pavilion, and a simulated shooting range, where you can test your eye coordination and shooting skills. Or you can try the even more challenging and exciting Crossfire Paintball. The On Location reporter will take you on a journey through Singapore's history and let you "report" on the nation's milestones.

iWERKS The iWERKS Theatre, next to the main exhibition hall, has a five-story-high screen and state-of-the-art sound system, and offers a truly unforgettable cinematic experience.

Singapore Nature Reserves

HIGHLIGHTS

Bukit Timah
- Macaques
- Strangler figs
- Bird hide

MacRitchie Reservoir Park
- TreeTop Walk
- Birdlife
- Macaques

Sungei Buloh
- Mangrove walkways
- Estuarine crocodiles
- Free guided tours on Saturday

TIP

- The macaques can be a real nuisance here, so resist the temptation to feed them and watch out that they don't snatch food from your hands.

Singapore is renowned for its green open spaces and, given its size, there are a surprising number of reserves where the original vegetation remains.

Bukit Timah The last remaining area of primary tropical rainforest in Singapore covers 410 acres (166ha) of Bukit Timah. Trails that start at the visitor area allow you to observe the reserve's fauna and flora. Lianas and rattans trail and twist through the forest, where you'll see huge strangler figs adorned with bird's nests and staghorn ferns.

MacRitchie Reservoir Park You can jog or walk on the shaded paths around the reservoir's edge; there are exercise stations at intervals. The highlight of several walks through the Park, the TreeTop Walk, is along a freestanding suspension bridge

Bukit Timah Nature Reserve (left); fungi on a tree stump at Bukit Timah Nature Reserve

THE BASICS

www.nparks.gov.sg

Bukit Timah

➕ b2

✉ 177 Hindhede Drive

☎ 1800 471 7300

🕐 Daily 8–6

🚍 MRT to Newton, then SBS bus 171 or TIBS 182, 65, 67, 75, 170, 171, 852, 961

♿ None

✋ Free

MacRitchie Reservoir Park

➕ c2

✉ Lornie road

🕐 24 hours

🍴 Food kiosk

🚍 MRT to Newton, then bus 104, 132 or 167

♿ Good

✋ Free

Sungei Buloh

➕ b1

✉ 301 Neo Tiew Crescent

☎ 6794 1401

🕐 7.30am–7pm Mon–Sat, 7am–7pm Sun and public holidays

🚍 Take SMRT Bus 925 from either Woodlands MRT Station or Kranji MRT Station

♿ Good

✋ Inexpensive

that connects the park's two highest points. From another bridge you can watch tortoises and carp and, if it's switched on, you'll see the fountain, which features 30 water-jet patterns. Concerts take place in the pavilion. Look for the long-tailed macaques, but don't go near them.

Sungei Buloh Singapore's only wetland nature reserve covers 217 acres (88ha). Carefully planned walkways allow you to explore swamp, mangrove and mudflat habitats, and to observe tropical birdlife and many species of marine creatures, particularly mudskippers and crabs. Early morning and evening are the best times for viewing wildlife, with bird life most evident before 10am. From September to March, the reserve is home to migratory birds from as far afield as eastern Siberia.

Singapore Science Centre

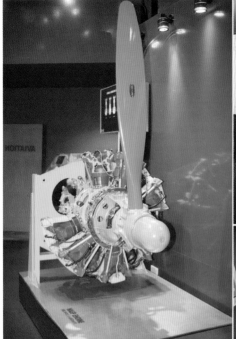

WEST ISLAND TOP 25

HIGHLIGHTS

- Atrium laser show
- Aviation Gallery
- Discovery Centre
- Ecogarden
- Omni Theatre

TIP

● The Science Centre shop has some excellent science kits and games for kids.

Hundreds of hands-on exhibits excite children and enlighten adults. The world of science and wonder awaits at the Singapore Science Centre, which houses more than 850 exhibits.

Interactive exhibits The Singapore Science Centre attracts more than a million visitors each year. Exhibits in themed galleries offer fascinating insights into human achievements in the physical and life sciences. Many of the exhibits are interactive, and some are supported by talks and films.

Science to hand A laser light display welcomes you in the main lobby. The Aviation Gallery, introduces the principles of flight and examines how man first explored the skies. The Life Sciences

Clockwise from left: Singapore Science Centre Aviation Gallery; a giant tongue at the Human Anatomy section; The World of Energy; the Atrium laser show; the robotics section and the human anatomy section

Gallery focuses on the environment and people. You can walk through the internal organs of a human body in the Human Anatomy section. The Discovery Centre aims to stimulate the imagination of younger children with interactive displays, and the Ecogarden is informative for horti-culturalists, with its mini-orchard, hydroponic farm and medicinal garden.

Omni Theatre and Planetarium Next to the Science Centre is the Omni Theatre. This theater has a five-floor high, 75ft (23m) curved Omnimax screen, and state-of-the-art projection and audio equipment with surround sound. You can see films on subjects as diverse as climbing Mt. Everest and the rule of China's first emperors. The features change every six months, so check to find out what's on during your visit.

THE BASICS

www.science.edu.sg

⊞ b3, A7

✉ 15 Science Centre Road

☎ 6425 2500

🕐 SSC Tue–Sun, public hols 10–6. Omni Theatre Tue–Sun, public hols 10–8

🍴 Café in SSC, fast food in Omni Theatre

🚇 Jurong East then 500 yards (500m) walk (turn left from station, along Block 135) or bus 335

🚌 66, 178, 198 direct; 51, 78, 197 to Jurong East Interchange then 335 or walk

♿ Good

💲 Inexpensive

Singapore Zoo

HIGHLIGHTS

- "Open" enclosures
- Tigers
- Pygmy hippos
- Primate islands
- Air-conditioned shelters
- Treetops Trail
- Komodo dragons
- Children's World
- Animal shows
- Tram

TIP

● Consider a Park Hopper 3-in-1 ticket for the zoo, Night Safari and Jurong BirdPark.

Treetops Trail, a wooden walkway 20ft (6m) off the ground, lets you join the gibbons and a troop of cheeky red langurs for a monkey's-eye view of a simulated rainforest.

Abandoned pets Singapore's zoo, acclaimed as one of the finest in the world, is also one of the youngest. Its beginnings can be traced back to the 1960s, when British forces pulled out of Singapore and left a ragbag of family pets behind. The zoo, which sprawls over 69 acres (28ha), was officially opened in 1973 and is now home to more than 290 species, some endangered and rare, such as tigers, orang-utans, Komodo dragons and golden lion tamarins. Breeding programs have been initiated for endangered species, with some success.

Clockwise from left: kangaroo feeding time; a giraffe; the tiger enclosure is one of the highlights; a young orang-utan; feeding time with the orang-utans; the zoo entrance and orang-utans with orchids

Polar bears and pygmy hippos Living conditions are as near as possible to those in the wild—mini-habitats bounded by naturalistic trenches, moats and rock walls. More than 2,050 animals can be seen. Polar bears, otters and pygmy hippos can be seen close up from underwater viewing areas, and the islands con-structed for the different primates provide a clear view of these generally hydrophobic creatures. The snake house is very popular with children and the tiger enclosure is always crowded. There is a great deal to see, and if you get tired of walking, you can always jump onto the silent tram that loops around the fine landscaped grounds, or take in one of the shows designed to entertain those not content with seeing sea lions, elephants and chimpanzees doing what comes naturally.

THE BASICS

www.zoo.com.sg
➕ C2, D1
✉ 80 Mandai Lake Road
☎ 6269 3411
🕐 Daily 8.30–6
🍴 Restaurants
🚇 MRT to Ang Mo Kio then SBS bus 138, or MRT to Choa Chu Kang then TIBS 927
🚌 SBS bus 171 to Mandai Road then cross road and take 138 or 927
♿ Good
💰 Moderate

More to See

CHINESE AND JAPANESE GARDENS

Chinese and Japanese classical gardens have been created on two islands in Jurong Lake. The Chinese Garden covers 32 acres (13ha) and is dotted with pagodas, pavilions and arched bridges. The main building is based on Beijing's Summer Palace. During the mid-autumn festival the gardens are hung with lanterns. The Japanese Gardens are altogether more serene, and take their inspiration from gardens of the 15th to 17th centuries.

➕ b3 ✉ 1 Chinese Garden Road ☎ 6261 3622 🕐 Daily 9am–11pm 🍴 Refreshment kiosks 🚇 Chinese Garden 💲 Inexpensive

COLONIAL RESIDENCES

A walk along Cluny, Lermit and Nassim roads, between the west end of Orchard Road and the Botanic Gardens, will give glimpses of 19th-century colonial residences. These mansions come equiped for making living in the tropical heat as tolerable as possible: enormous blinds, shaded balconies and verandas, and lush, landscaped gardens.

➕ A4, b4 ✉ Cluny, Lermit and Nassim roads 🚇 Orchard 💲 Free

HARBOURFRONT

The Harbourfront Precinct, which includes the Singapore Cruise Centre, spans 59 acres (24ha) along Singapore's southern waterfront at the foothills of Mount Faber, and overlooks the resort island of Sentosa (▷ 60). A popular destination, this former exhibition area has been transformed into a waterfront hub for work, living and recreation, as well as a great waterfront dining destination. Be sure to check out VivoCity (▷ 43), Singapore's largest shopping mall, and the city's latest entertainment area, St. James Power Station.

➕ B9, c4 ✉ 1 Maritime Square 🕐 7am–12midnight daily 🚇 Harbourfront

HAW PAR VILLA (TIGER BALM GARDENS)

This theme park, built in 1937, is based on Chinese myth and legend

Brightly painted statue at Haw Par Villa (left)

Bonsai Garden at the Chinese Gardens (below)

and real crimes in old Singapore. Brightly painted statues, boat rides, a 197ft (60m) long dragon and animated puppets will entertain children.

🟥 c3 ✉ 262 Pasir Panjang Road ☎ 6872 2720 🕐 Daily 9–7 🍴 Cafés 🚇 MRT Buona Vista then bus 200 💷 Free

KRANJI WAR MEMORIAL

The War Memorial is dedicated to the service personnel from Malaya, India, Sri Lanka, Australia, New Zealand, Britain and Canada who died defending Singapore and Malaya against the Japanese during World War II. More than 4,000 marked graves stand in rows along the well-kept lawns, and the names of those whose bodies were not recovered (over 24,000) are inscribed on the sides of the memorial's 12 walls. The cemetery, a hospital burial ground during the occupation, became a military cemetery after the war.

🟥 b1 ✉ 9 Woodlands Road 🕐 Daily 7am–6pm 🚌 SBS bus 170 from Rochor Road 🚇 Kranji Station 💷 Free

NUS CENTRE FOR THE ARTS

www.nus.edu.sg/museums
The Centre manages Singapore National University's three art collections. The Chinese art collection, located at lobby level in the Lee Kong Chian Art Museum, has six galleries of paintings, calligraphy, ceramics and bronze artefacts representing every major era of Chinese history. The South and Southeast Asian collection, at concourse level in the South and Southeast Asian Gallery, displays artworks that span classical to modern traditions in drawing and painting, textile, ceramics, sculptures and bronzes. The Ng Eng Teng collection, at the top level in the Ng Eng Teng Gallery, contains over 1,000 items—sculptures, vessels, ceramic forms, paintings and drawings—by Singapore's foremost sculptor.

🟥 b3 ✉ University Cultural Centre Annex, 50 Kent Ridge Crescent, National University of Singapore ☎ 6516 4617 🕐 Mon–Sat 10am–5pm 🚇 MRT to the Clementi Station, then bus number 96
💷 Free

Kranji War Memorial Cemetery (above)

Porcelain Buddha gilt-bronze mask, NUS Centre for the Arts (right)

A Walk through the Botanic Gardens

This walk takes you through the National Orchid Garden (▷ 52–53), so a good time to start is around opening hour—8.30am.

DISTANCE: 1–1.5 miles (1.5–2.5km) **ALLOW:** 2–3 hours

START

END

TANGLIN GATE (MAIN GATE)
🚇 A3, A4, c3 🚌 MRT to Orchard, then SBS Bus 7, 106, 123, 174

TANGLIN GATE OR VISITOR CENTRE

1 Take the path to the left that leads to the March Garden ponds. These lovely ponds, created out of a natural wetlands, feature local and non-native water plants.

2 Keep walking to the left around the ponds and follow some stepping stones. Take the turn to the right and walk along to Swan Lake, with its resident white swans and exuberant "Swing Me Mama" sculpture.

3 Continue walking straight ahead until several paths meet and you can see three sets of steps. Take the middle steps to the Sundial Garden—you'll see a Floral Clock on the far side.

4 Climb the steps to the left of the Floral Clock and turn left. Keep going and you'll reach the Sun Rockery, and a little farther on there is a display of the gorgeous Vanda "Miss Joaquim" orchid, the national flower of Singapore.

8 Walk downhill to leave the Orchid Gardens. Stroll down the lawn at Palm Valley and admire the palms, then relax by Symphony Lake, before walking up to the Visitor Centre.

7 Down the hill to the right you'll find a huge collection of bromeliads, and the Cool House nearby that houses tropical montane orchid species. From here you loop back up to the Orchidarium, with its lowland species.

6 A path from the Ginger Garden will take you directly to the Orchid Plaza and National Orchid Garden. Turn right once you're inside the gardens and walk to the fountain. Turn left here and walk uphill to the Tan Hoon Siang Mist House.

5 When you reach the end of the orchid display, you'll see an extremely tall forest tree—walk down the path at its side and along to the Ginger Garden, home to plants in the ginger family and related species.

WALK

WEST ISLAND

Shopping

ANTIQUES OF THE ORIENT

You could spend hours browsing through this shop's fine selection of old lithographs, prints, maps and books.
🔲 B4 ✉ 02-40 Tanglin Shopping Centre, 19 Tanglin Road ☎ 6734 9351
🕐 Mon–Sat 10–6, Sun 10.30–4.30 🚇 Orchard

BURMESE FINE ARTS

Specializes in Cambodian, Burmese and Thai arte-facts and curios. The rep-utable dealer offers certifi-cates of authenticity with each antique.
🔲 A4 ✉ 03-10 Holland Shopping Centre, Holland Village ☎ 6466 9089 🕐 Mon–Sat 10–6 🚌 7, 61, 106

HOLLAND ROAD SHOPPING CENTRE

Ethnic goods from all over Asia. Includes porce-lain, cloisonné, arts and crafts and clothing.
🔲 A4 ✉ 211 Holland Avenue ☎ 6338 8135 🕐 Daily 10–9 G5, 7, 61, 106

LIM'S ARTS & CRAFTS

Authentic handicrafts, including linens, jewelry, pottery and silk pyjamas.
🔲 A4 ✉ 02-01 Holland Road Shopping Centre, 211 Holland Avenue ☎ 6467 1300
🕐 Mon–Sat 9.30–8.30, Sun, public holidays 10.30–6.30 🚌 5, 7, 61, 106

MATA HARI ANTIQUES

The basketry, lacquerware and silver jewelry here originate from Thailand, Cambodia, Vietnam, Indonesia and Myanmar (Burma).
🔲 B4 ✉ 02-26 Tanglin Shopping Centre, 19 Tanglin Road ☎ 6737 6068
🚇 Orchard

SELECT BOOKS

This cozy bookshop car-ries Singapore's largest selection of books on Southeast Asia, with an extensive range of aca-demic texts, travel guides and coffee-table books.
🔲 B4 ✉ 03-15 Tanglin Shopping Centre, 19 Tanglin Road ☎ 6732 1515
🕐 Mon–Sat 9.30–6.30 🚇 Orchard

CARPET AUCTIONS

Taking in a carpet auction can be a fun way to spend a Sunday. Several carpet com-panies hold auctions then, usually at the Hyatt, the Hilton or the Holiday Inn. Carpets are spread out for easy viewing from about 10am until just after noon. Estimated market prices are posted and a Continental-type buffet breakfast is often free to participants. Auctions usually start about 1pm. Depending on the number of viewers and the size of their wallets, bidding proceeds at a fast pace. Expect to get 50–70 percent off the estimated price, or at least start the bidding there.

TANGLIN MALL

This shopping mall pro-vides something a little different from the design-er labels on offer else-where on Orchard Road. The range of stores includes some interesting children's shops, a sports shop and three floors of Food Junction. A handi-crafts market is held the third Saturday of every month.
🔲 B4 ✉ 163 Tanglin Road ☎ 6736 4922 🕐 Daily 10–10 🚇 Orchard

TANGLIN SHOPPING CENTRE

One of the area's oldest shopping malls, this is well known for its Asian antiques and curios (though, as elsewhere in Singapore, prices are high). It is also good for carpets, tailoring and cameras and accessories. Near the intersection of Tanglin and Orchard roads.
🔲 B4 ✉ 19 Tanglin Road ☎ 6737 0849 🕐 Daily 10–6 🚇 Orchard

TERESE JADE & MINERALS

Jade is a Chinese favorite. Check out the loose beads and stones—you can make your own jew-elry or have it custom made on the premises.
🔲 B4 ✉ 01-28 Tanglin Shopping Centre, 19 Tanglin Road ☎ 6734 0379
🕐 Mon–Sat 10–6 🚇 Orchard

Restaurants

PRICES

Prices are approximate, based on a 3-course meal for one person.

$$$	over S$50
$$	S$20–S$50
$	under S$20

COFFEE CLUB, HOLLAND VILLAGE ($)

The Coffee Club specializes in interesting coffees, some with cream and a choice of different spirits.

🔼 A4 ✉ 48 Lorong Mambong ☎ 6466 0296 🕐 Daily 10am–11pm 🚌 5, 7, 61, 106

LA FORKETTA ($$)

Although this Italian restaurant is a little off the beaten track it's worth the trip, as the food is delicious, particularly the first-class pizza.

🔼 D5 ✉ 491 River Valley Road ☎ 6836 3373 🕐 Daily 12–2.30, 6–10.30 🚌 14, 32, 54, 65, 139, 195

AL FORNO TRATTORIA ($$)

A popular restaurant, though a little way out of the heart of the city, so be sure to make a reservation. Antipasto and pizzas are particularly tasty.

🔼 D2 ✉ 203 Thomson Road ☎ 6256 2838 🕐 Daily 12–2, 6.30–10.30 🚇 Novena

MICHELANGELO'S ($$)

Innovative Italian cuisine from this multi-award-winning restaurant comes in generous portions served by professional staff. Dine among the fresco paintings or eat outside by candlelight.

🔼 A4 ✉ 01–60 Chip Bee Gardens, 44 Jalan Merah Saga ☎ 6475 9069 🕐 Mon–Sun 11–2.30, 6–10.30 🚌 7, 61, 106

ORIGINAL SIN ($$)

The menu at this Mediterranean-style restaurant is completely vegetarian. The imaginative use of ingredients gives run-of-the-mill dishes a real twist.

🔼 Off map to west ✉ Block 43, Jalan Merah Saga, 01–62

COFFEE SHOPS

Singapore's traditional coffee shops are nothing like the modern places that sell a sophisticated selection of Javanese coffee and brownies. They are no-nonsense, cheap and cheerful options for popular local rice and noodle dishes. You also get coffee, but it's thick and sweet, made with condensed milk. Mindful of waste, coffee shops sometimes serve take-out coffee in empty condensed-milk cans, and you will occasionally see people carrying these, though the more usual coffee container today is the familiar Styrofoam container or a plastic bag, which you can sometimes see tied to railings while the contents cool.

Chip Bee Gardens, Holland Village ☎ 6475 5605 🕐 Tue–Sun 11–2.30, 6–10.30 🚌 5, 7, 61, 106

ROCKY'S ($$)

If you feel like ordering pizza to eat in, Rocky's is the place. You need to allow about an hour for delivery.

🔼 Off map to north ✉ 392 Upper Bukit Timah Road ☎ 6468 9188 🕐 Daily 11–10.30 (last order 10) 🚌 No public transport

SAMY'S CURRY ($)

Located in a private civil-service clubhouse, with a colonial edifice and overhead fans; meals here are served on banana leaves. Try spoonfuls of zesty curries, fragrant rices, breads and assorted condiments. You must get $2 temporary membership to the Singapore Civil Service Club to eat here, but don't let this put you off.

🔼 A4 ✉ Singapore Civil Service Club House, Block 25, Dempsey Road ☎ 6472 2080 🕐 Mon–Wed 11–2.30, 6–10, Thu–Sun 11–2.30, 6–10 🚇 Orchard

SISTINA ($)

Great family destination offers 20 different pizza styles and countless pasta combinations.

🔼 A4 ✉ 01–58 Chip Bee Gardens, 44 Jalan Merah Saga, Holland Village ☎ 6476 7782 🕐 Lunch daily, lunch and dinner Sat, Sun 🚌 7, 61, 106

The east of Singapore boasts long, sandy beaches lined with excellent seafood restaurants, recreational water sports, including a cable ski park, poignant World War II memorials and historical temples.

Sights	78–87	Top 25	**25**
Walk	88	Changi Chapel and Museum ▷ **78**	
Shopping	90	Joo Chiat Road ▷ **79**	
		East Coast Park ▷ **80–81**	
Entertainment and Nightlife	91	Republic of Singapore Air Force Museum ▷ **82–83**	
Restaurants	92	Siong Lim Temple ▷ **84**	

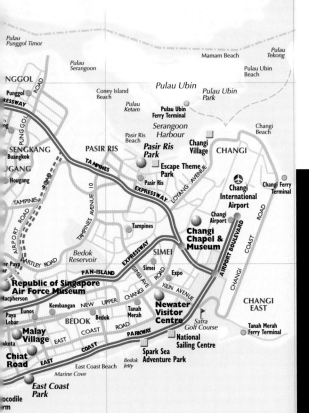

MY

Pulau
Punggol Timor

Pulau
Serangoon

Mamam Beach

Pulau
Tekong

Pulau Ubin
Beach

NGGOL

Punggol

ESSWAY

Coney Island
Beach

Pulau
Ketam

Pulau Ubin

Pulau Ubin
Park

Changi
Beach

Serangoon
Harbour

Pulau Ubin
Ferry Terminal

SENGKANG
Buangkok

PASIR RIS

Pasir Ris
Beach

Pasir Ris
Park

Changi
Village

CHANGI

UGANG
Hougang

TAMPINES

Escape Theme
Park

Pasir Ris

EXPRESSWAY

LOYANG AVENUE

Changi
International
Airport

Changi Ferry
Terminal

TAMPINES

ROAD

TAMPINES AVENUE 10

AIRPORT ROAD

BARTLEY ROAD

Tampines

Bedok
Reservoir

EXPRESSWAY

Changi
Airport

SIMEI

Changi
Chapel &
Museum

AIRPORT BOULEVARD

CHANGI ROAD

er Paya

PAN-ISLAND

Simei

Road

Expo

Republic of Singapore
Air Force Museum

Macpherson

Kembangan

NEW

UPPER

CHANGI

SIMEI AVE

XILIN AVENUE

CHANGI
EAST

Paya
Lebar

Eunos

BEDOK

Bedok

Tanah
Merah

Newater
Visitor
Centre

Safra
Golf Course

Malay
Village

EAST

COAST

ROAD

PARKWAY

Tanah Merah
Ferry Terminal

akota

Chiat
Road

EAST

COAST

National
Sailing Centre

Marine Cove

East Coast Beach

Bedok
Jetty

Spark Sea
Adventure Park

East Coast
Park

ocodile
rm

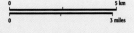

0   5 km
0   3 miles

Changi Chapel and Museum

TOP 25

The Changi Chapel (left) and the museum chapel memorial wall (right)

THE BASICS

🔲 e2
✉ 1000 Upper Changi Road North
☎ 6214 2451
🕐 Daily 9.30–4.30
🚇 Tanah Merah. Take SBS bus 2 from station
🎟 Free

HIGHLIGHTS

● Replica Murals
● Video screenings
● Wartime plants

During World War II, some 50,000 civilians, Allied troops and prisoners were incarcerated in Singapore. Exhibits at the Changi Prison Chapel and Museum portray the terrible conditions they endured —some for more than three years.

Fitting memorial Housed within the open-air courtyard of the museum, the Changi Chapel is a reconstruction of one of the many chapels built at Changi Prison during the Japanese Occupation. This poignant monument to those who strived to maintain their faith during their years in captivity is a fitting memorial to all who were imprisoned.

Changi Murals The museum displays photographs, letters, drawings and personal effects of some of the tens of thousands of civilians, soldiers and other war prisoners. There is also a replica of the original Changi Murals, which were painted by bombardier Stanley Warren. Visitors are welcome to join the 9am Sunday services, conducted by various church groups at the Changi Chapel.

"Elizabeth Choy" There are regular screenings of videos such as "Changi Through The Eyes of Haxworth" about a prisioner whose sketches vividly capture his years in Changi, and "Elizabeth Choy", the story of a civilian heroine who withstood nearly 200 days of imprisonment and torture. Tours are available from 10am, with the last tour at 3.45pm. There is a café and the garden has a collection of plants that Singapore residents typically planted during the Japanese Occupation.

A shop display on Joo Chiat Road (left) and terraced houses (right)

Joo Chiat Road

Wonderful original architecture and intriguing old businesses by day, and an exciting mix of restaurants and music lounges in the evening, give a fascinating glimpse of former times and a sample of Singapore life today.

History This once quiet seaside village is today an eclectic mix of colonial villas, Peranakan-style terraces and Malay bungalows. Some are preserved, many are being renovated, others remain untouched. The Joo Chiat Complex, at the northern end of Joo Chiat near the Malay Village, is a busy local shopping complex selling fabrics and household goods at bargain prices. Next to the Village is the Geylang Serai market, a traditional Asian market, a good place to browse.

Eclectic mix Opposite Guan Hoe Soon Restaurant (which serves traditional Peranakan nonya dishes) is a typical 1920s corner terrace, with an ornate frieze of green dragons on the roof pediment. Terrace houses with covered walkways can be found along the road. The second floors may be pillared verandas (No. 113), or have ornate casement windows (Nos. 370–76). Colorful tiles are a common feature (Nos. 137–39). Koon Seng Road, to the left, has two rows of terrace houses with courtyard gardens in front and extravagant moldings, tiles and paintwork. Set in dense gardens are Malay-style bungalows (Nos. 229, 382) fronted by verandas flanked by staircases. Villas to the southern end (Nos. 507–509) indicate that this was the seafront before land reclamation.

THE BASICS

+ d3
- Joo Chiat Road
- Guan Hoe Soon 6344 2761. Katong Antique House 6345 8544
- Guan Hoe Soon (nonya food, No. 214); Casa Bom Vento (No. 47); Mum's Kitchen (No. 314); AJ Tandoori's (No. 328); Lemongrass (899 East Coast Road)
- Paya Lebar then walk
- 16, 33
- None
- Free

HIGHLIGHTS

- Guan Hoe Soon Restaurant
- Joo Chiat Complex
- Katong Antique House
- Koon Seng Road
- Malay Village
- Malay-style bungalows
- Old seafront luxury villas
- Peranakan-style shophouses
- Residential terraces

EAST ISLAND

TOP 25

East Coast Park

- Big Splash water rides
- Canoe rental
- East Coast Sailing Centre
- Parkland Golf Driving Range
- Tennis center
- SKI360

TIP

- Singapore's freshest seafood can be found at many of the waterfront eateries, but avoid Sunday, when they are always packed out.

Two decades of land reclamation have created this beachside playground. Swim or sail; walk, jog or cycle the 6 miles (10km) of tracks between coconut groves; or laze on white sands.

Plenty to do Picnicking families flock to the area on the weekends. There are many places to rent a bicycle, canoe, rollerblades or a deck chair, and it's a pleasant place to relax and catch a cooling breeze in the evening. The seafood center at the Urban Development and Management Corporation (UDMC) clubhouse is popular with those who appreciate good seafood. There are many other seafood dining places and the best way to choose one of these is to arrive before lunch or dinner time and stroll along the pathways checking out those that serve your favorite dishes.

Clockwise from left: A beach scene at East Coast Park; a lone bicycle on the beach; enjoying a picnic bbq; the cable ski park; you can also rent bicycles here

East Coast Sailing Centre Sailboards and laser dinghies can be rented here. If you encounter difficulties at sea, a rescue boat is on hand to bring you back to the East Coast Sailing Centre.

Marina Cove Next to the park at Marina Cove are clay tennis courts (open until late evening), a cable ski park (SKI360), where an overhead cable pulls you across the water at speeds of up to 37mph (60km/h). Golfers can practice at the two-tier, 163-yard (150m) Parkland for just the cost of the balls. You can also rent bicycles, rollerblades and canoes. At the Big Splash, water rides delight adults and children alike.

Beaches The 12 miles (20km) of beaches are popular on weekends, but swimming in the often murky waters is not advised.

THE BASICS

🔂 d3, L5, M5

✉ East Coast Service Road

☎ ECSC 6449 5118. Tennis Centre 6243 1792. Parkland Golf Range 6440 6726. Big Splash 6345 1321. SKI360 6442 7318

🍴 East Coast Lagoon Food Centre hawker center (▷ 92), various kiosks, fast food at Marina Cove and Big Splash

🚇 Bedok then bus 401 or bus 31, 197; Eunos then 55, 155; Paya Lebar then 76, 135 and walk

🚌 16, 31, 55, 76, 135, 155, 196, 197, 853 daily to Marine Parade Road; 401 to East Coast Service Road (Sun)

♿ Some level paths

💵 Free; rental charges per hour for sports, etc.

Republic of Singapore Air Force Museum

HIGHLIGHTS

- Bloodhound missile
- Hawker hunter
- A4-S Skyhawk
- Flight Simulator

TIP

- There really is a lot to see here for the aeronautically minded, so be sure to put aside plenty of time for this museum.

Get a fascinating insight into the history of aviation and the Royal Singapore Air Force and view a wide range of aircraft, from an early Cessna to the more recent A4-S Skyhawk.

History of aviation On the first level, the museum has a "History of Aviation" gallery, which displays new technologies and aircraft design, and tracks the development of aviation. There is also an Outdoor Gallery on this level. Information technology is used extensively throughout the museum. In all the galleries, soundscapes, videos and animations greatly enhance the exhibitions. A comfortable, state-of-the-art theatrette screens several multimedia productions on the RSAF and aviation in general, which will help get your mind in the zone before you tour the galleries.

Clockwise from top left: The Air Force Museum Modern Technology section; detail of ammunition rounds; a model of the first helicopter; medals on display; an ejector seat and a cockpit control panel

Indoor Galleries On the second level are eight indoor galleries where you'll learn about the history of the RSAF, see models of past and present aircraft, radar and weapons systems, and an interactive model of the Tengah Air Base, including a mock-up of a typical 1970s office. Gallery 4 features a Bloodhound missile and an interactive model of the Launch Control Post. Would-be pilots will enjoy the Flight Simulator diorama in Gallery 5.

Outdoor Gallery From the viewing deck on the second level there's a panoramic view of the aircraft in the Outdoor Gallery. The display includes early acquisitions of the RSAF, such as the Cessna 173K, BAC 167 Strikemaster and T-33 Shooting Star trainers. Later models on show include the Hawker Hunter, a single-seat fighter/ground attack aircraft used from the 1960s to the 1990s.

THE BASICS

www.mindef.gov.sg/rsaf/
about/te-afm.asp
⊞ d3
✉ 400 Airport Road
☎ 6461 8504/8506
🕐 Tue–Sun 8.30–5
🍴 Cafeteria
🚌 SBS 90 and 94 (SBS 90
not available on Sun)
🎟 Free

Siong Lim Temple

The beautiful exterior (left) and the elaborate interior (middle, right and opposite)

This Buddhist temple in Toa Payoh, set amid HDB residential towers, is a national monument to Singapore's Chinese immigrants.

Golden light Also known as the Lian Shan Shuang Lin Temple, it was built between 1868 and 1908 on land donated by Low Kim Pong, a wealthy Chinese Hokkien merchant. He was inspired by his dream of a golden light rising over the sea from the west, which he took to be a Buddhist omen. Next day, he went to the coast and met a Hokkien family stopping over in their boat on their way home to Fujian in China, after a pilgrimage to Sri Lanka. Impressed by their devotion, Low promised to build a temple for their use if they would stay in Singapore. Xian Hui, the head of that family, was to become the first abbot.

Amalgamation of styles With designs based on the Xichang temple in Fujian province, the final building incorporated elements of the building styles of Fuzhou, Quanzhou and Zhangzhou, from where the original temple builders came. The temple is guarded by the giant Four Kings of Heaven, in full armor. The elaborately decorated gateway, reached by a bridge, opens into a courtyard, where there are several shrines and halls, with many beautifully carved features and statues of Buddha. In another hall, you'll see Thai Buddha images. The seven-floor gold-topped pagoda is a replica of the one at the 800-year-old Shanfeng temple in Fujian. The oldest building, a small wooden shrine, contains old murals of the much-loved Chinese legend "Pilgrimage to the West".

More to See

BISHAN HDB ESTATE

More than 84 percent of Singapore's population lives in state-subsidized Housing and Development Board apartments known as HDBs. Hundreds of these government-built blocks exist in any given area, each a small town in its own right. Bishan, developed in the early 1990s, adds to the steadily growing list of these distinctive housing estates. As with most HDB areas, it has its own MRT station, around which a shopping and entertainment complex, Junction 8, has been built. Wander around Junction 8's central area close to the MRT station, up Bishan Road, and from there turn right in front of the MRT, then left into Street 22. You'll come upon one of the many smaller satellite community areas, complete with its own shops and hawker center at the base of the housing blocks. On the outskirts of Bishan, at Bright Hill Drive, is Phor Kark See, a huge Buddhist temple overlooking Bishan Park.

✚ c2 ✉ Bishan Central 🍴 3rd Mini Steamboat Delight, 9 Bishan Place, 04–01G and numerous other coffee shops, hawker centers and fast-food outlets 🚇 Bishan 🚌 13, 53, 54, 55, 56, 156 ♿ Few 💲 Free

CENTRAL SIKH TEMPLE

This temple is the principal place of worship for Singapore's Sikh population. Its seven-floor tower houses the community facilities, which include a library, museum, a small dormitory and rooms for tourists. The magnificent prayer hall, covered by a 43ft (13m) -high dome, can accommodate up to 500 people. The modern main building is constructed of Sardinian pink granite, and the dome is covered with gold, and white and grey mosaics on the inside, and white mosaic tiles on the outside.

✚ G2, d3 ✉ 2 Towner Road ☎ 6299 3855 🕐 Daily 9–8 🚇 Boon Keng 💲 Free

MALAY VILLAGE

The Malays, the native inhabitants of Singapore, were dispersed by the British from the mouth of the Singapore River in the 1840s and moved to the area now known as

Central Sikh Temple interior painting

Geylang. Descendants of that community, along with a large population of Indonesians, now live there. Geylang is a fascinating area to visit, especially during the Muslim religious holidays. The Malay Village complex features aspects of Malay culture and history, while the nearby Geylang Serai Market is a huge traditional Asian market, crammed with small stalls selling items used by a Malay household, clothings, textiles and crafts, and right at the end is a hawker food center with delicious ethnic dishes and local drinks. The wet market is incredible! You can visit a traditional kampong to see how the Malays lived in the 1950s and 1960s, and try your hand at traditional Malay crafts and games. ✚ d3 ✉ 39 Geylang Serai ☎ 6748 4700 🕐 10–10 🚇 Paya Lebar 🖐 Free to the village; Kampung Days and Cultural Museum, adults S$5, children S$3

NEWATER VISITOR CENTRE
www.pub.gov.sg
Learn how waste water is recycled into drinking water. Your virtual guide "Wave" explains each step of the process whereby dual-membrane (microfiltration and reverse osmosis) and ultraviolet technologies purify water to then return to Singapore's main water supply. Multimedia presentations and hands-on interactive games further explain this futuristic process. As well, you get the opportunity to feel, touch and taste the final product. ✚ e3 ✉ 20 Koh Sek Lim Road 🕐 6546 7874 🚇 Tanah Merah 🚌 12, 24, 31, 38 ♿ Good 🖐 Free

PASIR RIS PARK
This 175-acre (71ha) area contains some of Singapore's last remaining stretches of mangrove swamp, and is now a bird and nature reserve. Raised boardwalks meander through this habitat. Look for fiddler crabs, mudskippers and small-clawed otters. Birds you might spot include herons, yellow-vented bulbuls, brown-throated sunbirds and collared kingfishers. ✚ e2 ✉ Off Jalan Loyang Kecil 🕐 24 hours 🚇 MRT to Pasir Ris then bus 403 🖐 Free

Pasir Ris Park mangrove boardwalk (above)

Pony rides at Pasir Ris Park (right)

East Coast Park Walk

This recreational park (▷ 80–81) running for 12 miles (20km) along the East Coast, has water sports and seafood restaurants.

DISTANCE: 1–1.5 miles (1.5–2.5km) **ALLOW:** 2–3 hours

START

BUS STOP
🚏 e3 🚌 Bedok then 401, or 31, 197; Eunos then 55, 155, 196 to Marine Crescent and Marine Terrace

1 Walk to the lagoon, where you can watch cable-skiers of all ages practice their wakeboarding skills at SKI360°. Bring your bathing suit and have a go!

2 When you're finished, head north up the beach to the East Coast Lagoon Food Centre, a popular hawker centre, for a cool, fresh tropical fruit drink and an exotic snack.

3 Continue on up the beach to the nearby Pasta Fresca Sea Sports Centre and rent a sailboat or a sailboard or just sit in the shade and watch the action.

END

BUS STOP

6 Take a walk farther down the beach or a quiet nap under a beach-side coconut tree before you return to the bus stop for the trip back to the Bedok Interchange.

5 By now you should have worked up a real appetite, so head south down the beach to the East Coast Seafood Centre, where there are eight restaurants specializing in seafood. Try the local favorites—crispy baby octopus, drunken prawns and chilli crab—wonderful!

4 If there's not much wind, you can rent a dinghy a bit farther up the beach and row to the nearby Bedok Jetty, which is popular with recreational fisherfolk.

WALK

EAST ISLAND

Shopping

APOLLO GOLDSMITHS

One of many shops that sells gold jewelry along Buffalo Road and Serangoon Road. Gold is sold by the gram, so any difference in cost is due to the design and work.
🔆 F5 ✉ 01–08, Blk 664 Buffalo Road ☎ 6296 1838 🕐 Daily 10.30–8.30 🚇 Bugis

BATIK EMPORIUM

Leather, briefcases, camera cases and purses, as well as batik shirts, dresses and sarongs.
🔆 F4 ✉ 138 Arab Street ☎ 6294 7559 🕐 Mon–Sat 10–7.30, Sun 12–6.30 🚇 Bugis

CHANGI VILLAGE

Specialty shops in a village atmosphere. Everything at bargain prices: electronic equipment, shoes, batik dresses, Indian cotton clothing, kimonos, and carpets.
🔆 e2 ✉ North of Changi Airport 🚇 Tanah Merah, then take SBS bus no.2

INDIAN BAZAAR

In Indian bazaar fashion, this shop is bursting with textile, mats, saris, posters, craftworks and furniture.
🔆 F6 ✉ 07–09 High Street Plaza, 77 High Street ☎ 6336 6242 🕐 Daily 10–9 🚇 City Hall

LAVANYA ARTS

Textiles, small carvings, traditional furniture and jewelry are among the offerings in this excellent specialty Indian shop.
🔆 F6 ✉ 02–11–16 Excelsior Hotel and Shopping Centre, 5 Coleman Street ☎ 6339 9400 🕐 Mon–Sat 11.30–7 🚇 City Hall

MALAY VILLAGE

Located in the heart of Geylang, this collection of Malay buildings show cases local talent and houses an interesting range of objects.
🔆 d3, L3 ✉ 39 Geylang Serai ☎ 6748 4700 🕐 Daily 10–10 🚇 Paya Lebar

PARCO BUGIS JUNCTION

An interesting glass-covered shopping street with shophouses, modern

ANTIQUES

Furniture and artefacts over 100 years old, considered antiques, are sold in a plethora of antique and reproduction shops. Buy only from reputable dealers. They will give a certificate of antiquity or a detailed description along with a receipt. This proof may be required to ensure duty-free importation to the US and UK. Prices are usually lower in the country of origin than in Singapore; they vary widely here, and bargaining is essential.

retail outlets, a movie theater, and the Japanese department store, Seiyu.
🔆 F5 ✉ 200 Bugis Junction ☎ 6334 8831 🚇 Bugis

POPPY FABRIC

All the colors of the rainbow are represented in the lovely Thai and Chinese silks in this store and in other stores specializing in textiles along fascinating Arab Street.
🔆 F4 ✉ 111 Arab Street ☎ 6296 6352 🕐 Mon–Sat 10–6.15 🚇 Bugis

SIM LIM SQUARE

Several floors of shops sell a large variety of electronic goods, including appliances, computers, software and televisions. Look for the red "Merlion" logo that indicates a "Good Retailer" approved by the STB (▷ 11).
🔆 F5 ✉ 1 Rochor Canal Road ☎ 6336 3922 🕐 Daily 10.30am–11pm (individual shops' hours may vary) 🚇 Bugis

THANDAPANI CO

This traditional provisions shop specializes in spices used in Indian cooking.
🔆 F5 ✉ 124 Dunlop Street ☎ 6292 3163 🕐 Daily 9–9 🚇 Bugis

Entertainment and Nightlife

ASOKA MUSIC LOUNGE

This Indian bar plays hip-hop and Bollywood soundtracks, and has live music after 9pm nightly.

✠ e2 ✉ 360 Balestier Road, 04-01 Shaw Plaza ☎ 6345 2519 Ⓞ Kallang ➍ 21, 130, 131, 145, 186

CHANGI SAILING CLUB

Although a private club and a long way out of town, this makes a lovely, relaxing place for an evening drink and meal, which can be taken on the small balcony overlooking the beach, under the palm trees or in the comfortable bar. Non-members are admitted for a dollar Monday to Friday evenings.

✠ e3 ✉ 32 Netheravon Road ☎ 6545 2876 Ⓞ Restaurant: daily 10–10 Ⓠ MRT to Tampines then bus 29

DOWNTOWN EAST

www.downtowneast.com.sg
Lots of entertainment choices at affordable prices: theme parks, resorts, food courts, retail shopping, gaming areas and a children's play area.

✠ e2 ✉ Pasir Ris Drive 3, next to Pasir Ris Park ☎ 6589 1688 Ⓞ Daily 9am until late Ⓠ Pasir Ris, then take the Shuttle Bus

THE DUBLINER IRISH PUB

Set in a former colonial mansion, this popular pub, with its plush interior, serves excellent food.

✠ E5 ✉ 165 Penang Road ☎ 6735 2220 Ⓞ Daily noon–2am Ⓠ Dhoby Ghaut

DXO

www.dxo.com.sg
Offers cheap beer and an outdoor view of the Marina Promenade from The Nest, where you can chill out and enjoy Retro, R&B and the commercial Top 40s.

✠ F6 ✉ 8 Raffles Avenue, Esplanade Mall Ⓞ Daily 5pm until late ☎ 6582 4896 Ⓠ Millenia

INDIAN DANCE

Singapore's Indian population takes its dance very seriously, and local dance academies put on public performances. The exacting steps and hand gestures, the exciting rhythms and the brilliant costumes of dance forms such as *orissi* are an

DANCE CLUBS

Like elsewhere, Singapore dance clubs tend to suit particular groups of revelers. While expats can be found at such places as Harry's Quayside and Papa Joe's, the mostly young locals find Europa Music Underground (▷ 44) and Lox (▷ 45) suit their tastes . Cover charges range from S$12 to S$25 and usually include one drink.

unusual delight and well worth checking out.

Nrityalaya Aesthetics Society
✠ F5 ✉ 155 Waterloo Street ☎ 6336 6537 Ⓠ Bugis

KALLANG NETBALL CENTRE

This modern facility is in the grounds of the National Stadium. There are six courts here but you should call ahead.

✠ J4, d3 ✉ 52 Stadium Blvd ☎ 6348 1291 Ⓞ Daily 7am–10pm Ⓠ Kallang

KALLANG THEATRE

This is Singapore's largest theater; it is here that crowd-pulling shows from around the world, such as Cats, are staged.

✠ J5, d3 ✉ 1 Stadium Walk ☎ 6345 8488 Ⓠ City Hall ➍ 16

OD'S BACKSTAGE MUSIC BAR

Great jazz and R&B, played by OD Levy and his band, and delicious finger food from the Italian restaurant next door.

✠ J5 ✉ 01-07 Kallang Indoor Stadium, 2 Stadium Walk ☎ 6342 5303 Ⓞ Mon–Fri 6pm–12midnight; Sat, Sun 6pm–2am Ⓠ Stadium Boulevard

TAMPINES STADIUM ROCK CLIMBING WALL

This excellent wall is one of the many in Singapore.

✠ d2 ✉ 25 Tampines Street ☎ 6781 1980 Ⓞ Daily 9am–11pm Ⓠ Tampines

Restaurants

PRICES

Prices are approximate, based on a 3-course meal for one person.
$$$ over S$50
$$ S$20–S$50
$ under S$20

BANANA LEAF APOLLO ($$)

A southern Indian "banana-leaf" restaurant where the leaf takes the place of a plate—with a good range of dishes to accompany the vegetable curries.

F4 ☒ 56 Race Course Road ☎ 6293 8682 ⏰ Daily 10.30–10 🚇 Little India

CHIN WAH HENG SEAFOOD ($$)

Popular dishes, including Chili Crab, are on the menu at this long-established East Coast restaurant. Kids are especially welcome here.

M5 ☒ 01–01 East Coast Seafood Centre, Block 1202 East Coast Parkway ☎ 6444 7967 ⏰ Daily 5pm–midnight 🚇 Eunos, then bus 55 or 105 🚌 16, 55, 76, 135, 155

COLOURS BY THE BAY ($$)

A novel dining experience, since it brings together many cuisines under one roof, from Chinese to Korean, Thai, Italian and fusion.

F6 ☒ 1–13A/G Esplanade Mall, 8 Raffles Avenue ☎ 6341 9985 ⏰ Daily 11.30–2.30; 6–11 🚇 Millenia

EAST COAST LAGOON FOOD CENTRE ($)

The good food and sea breezes make this popular. The satay is very good, as are the *laksa* and any number of tantalizing seafood dishes, including chili or black pepper crab.

d3 ☒ East Coast Parkway ⏰ Late morning until late daily 🚇 Bugis, then bus 401 (Sat, Sun, holidays only)

IMPERIAL HERBAL RESTAURANT ($$$)

Ants and scorpions, anyone? You'll find them on the menu here.

F5 ☒ Metropole Hotel, 41 Seah Street ☎ 6337 0491 ⏰ Daily 11.30–2.30, 6.30–10.30 🚇 City Hall

JUMBO SEAFOOD ($$$)

Lots of tasty seafood dishes, but renown for its chili crab.

d3 ☒ 1208 East Coast Parkway ☎ 6442 3435 ⏰ Daily 11.30–2, 6–11 🚇 Eunos, then bus 55 or 105 🚌 16, 55, 76, 135, 155

STEAMBOAT

Not a form of transportation, rather a delicious method of tableside cooking where a selection of fish, meat and vegetables is placed in a container of boiling broth; you can cook it to your liking and retrieve it with chopsticks when it's achieved perfect readiness.

LEI GARDEN ($$$)

The CHIJMES branch of this upscale chain serves Cantonese specialties such as Beijing duck.

F5 ☒ 01–24 Chijmes, 30 Victoria Street ☎ 6339 3822 ⏰ Daily 11.30– 2.30, 6–10.30 🚇 City Hall

MANGO TREE ($$)

Popular beachside location and delicious southern Indian cuisine, plus sunset views.

d3 ☒ 1000 East Coast Parkway ☎ 6442 8655 ⏰ Daily 11.30–2.30, 6.30–11 🚇 Eunos, then bus 55 or 105 🚌 16, 55, 76, 135, 155

SKETCHES PASTA & WINE BAR ($)

Set around the kitchen, the idea of this friendly place is that you design your own pasta dishes from a list of fresh ingredients.

F5 ☒ 200 Victoria Street, 01–85 Parco Bugis Junction ☎ 6339 8386 ⏰ Daily 11–10 🚇 Bugis

WAK LOK CANTONESE RESTAURANT ($$)

Fine Cantonese dinners and tasty dim sum lunches. Hong Kong Chinese come here to eat.

F5 ☒ Carlton Hotel, 76 Bras Basah Road ☎ 6311 8188 ⏰ Mon–Sat 11.30–2.30, 6.30–10.30, Sun 11–2.30, 6.30–10.30 🚇 City Hall

Singapore is so close to exciting Malaysian and Indonesian destinations that, if you have time, you should experience the exotic differences offered by some of the cities, ports and resorts of the area.

Sights	96–99	Top 25	**25**
Diving Singapore's Islands	100–101	Pulau Ubin ▷ **96–97**	
Excursions	102–103		
Walk	104		
Shopping	105		
Restaurants	105		

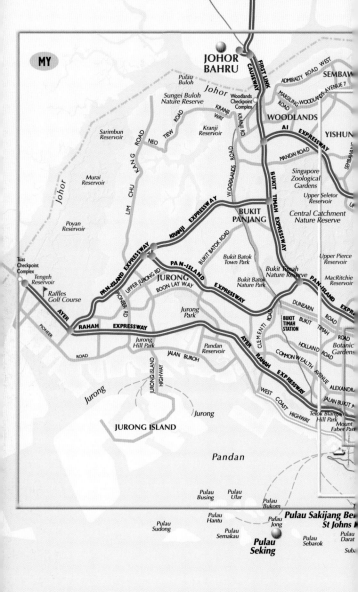

MY

JOHOR BAHRU

FIRST LINK CAUSEWAY

ADMIRALTY ROAD WEST

Johor

Pulau Buloh

SEMBAW

Sungei Buloh Nature Reserve

Woodlands Checkpoint Complex

MARSLING-WOODLANDS ROAD

MARSLING ROAD

KRANJI WAY

WOODLANDS

YISHUN

Kranji Reservoir

KRANJI RD

AI EXPRESSWAY

NEO TIEW ROAD

SEMBAWAN

Sarimbun Reservoir

LIM CHU KANG ROAD

MANDAI ROAD

WOODLANDS ROAD

Singapore Zoological Gardens

Murai Reservoir

Upper Seletor Reservoir

BUKIT TIMAH EXPRESSWAY

BUKIT PANJANG

Central Catchment Nature Reserve

Poyan Reservoir

Johor

KRANJI EXPRESSWAY

BUKIT BATOK ROAD

Bukit Batok Town Park

Upper Pierce Reservoir

PAN-ISLAND EXPRESSWAY

Bukit Timah Nature Reserve

Bukit Batok Nature Park

MacRitchie Reservoir

Tuas Checkpoint Complex

Tengeh Reservoir

UPPER JURONG RD

BOON LAY WAY

PAN-ISLAND EXPRESSWAY

JURONG

PAN-ISLAND EXPRE

Raffles Golf Course

PIONEER RD

E EXPRESSWAY

DUNEARN

ROAD

AYER

PAN-ISLAND EXPRESSWAY

Jurong Park

CLEMENTI RD

BUKIT TIMAH

PIONEER

RAHAH EXPRESSWAY

BUKIT TIMAH STATION

ROAD

Botanic Gardens

ROAD

Jurong Hill Park

Pandan Reservoir

JALAN BUROH

HOLLAND ROAD

COMMONWEALTH AVENUE

JURONG ISLAND HIGHWAY

AYER RAHAH EXPRESSWAY

ALEXANDRA

Jurong

Jurong

WEST COAST HIGHWAY

JALAN BUKIT M

Telok Blangah Hill Park

Mount Faber Pa

JURONG ISLAND

Pandan

Pulau Busing

Pulau Ular

Pulau Bukom

Pulau Hantu

Pulau Jong

Pulau Sakijang Be St Johns I

Pulau Sudong

Pulau Semakau

Pulau Seking

Pulau Sebarok

Pulau Darat

Suba

0   5 km

0   3 miles

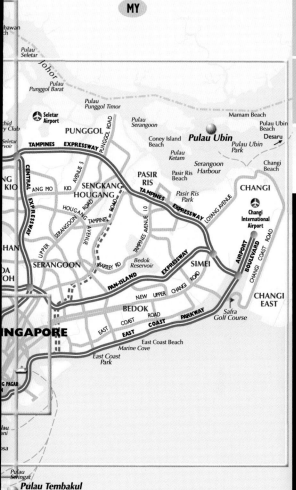

MY

Pulau
Seletar

Johor

Pulau
Punggol Barat

Pulau
Punggol Timor

Mamam Beach

Seletar
Airport

PUNGGOL

Pulau
Serangoon

Pulau Ubin
Beach

Coney Island
Beach

Pulau Ubin

Desaru

TAMPINES   EXPRESSWAY

Pulau Ubin
Park

Pulau
Ketam

PUNGGOL ROAD

Serangoon
Harbour

Changi
Beach

PASIR
RIS

Pasir Ris
Beach

AVENUE 5

SENGKANG
HOUGANG

TAMPINES

Pasir Ris
Park

CHANGI

ANG MO KIO

HOUGANG ROAD

TAMPINES AVENUE

TAMPINES AVENUE 10

EXPRESSWAY

LOYANG AVENUE

Changi
International
Airport

SERANGOON ROAD

CENTRAL   EXPRESSWAY

UPPER SERANGOON ROAD

SERANGOON

BARTLEY RD

Bedok
Reservoir

EXPRESSWAY

SIMEI
ROAD

AIRPORT   BOULEVARD

CHANGI COAST ROAD

PAN-ISLAND

NEW   UPPER   CHANGI   ROAD

CHANGI
EAST

BEDOK

EAST   COAST   ROAD

Safra
Golf Course

EAST   COAST   PARKWAY

INGAPORE

EAST   COAST

East Coast Beach

Marine Cove

East Coast
Park

PAGAR

Pulau
Seringat

Pulau Tembakul
Kusu

Pulau Sakijang Pelepah
Lazarus

Farther Afield

Pulau Ubin

HIGHLIGHTS

● Groves of coconuts
● Old rubber plantation
● Mangrove swamps

TIP

● Be sure to take insect repellent and sunscreen, as well as a good hat.

This undeveloped island just northeast of the mainland is a rural idyll compared to the concrete and consumerism of Singapore. You can wander through coconut groves and even mangrove swamps.

Eating and drinking Just off the jetty at Pulau Ubin there is an endearingly scruffy little village where you can enjoy Malay and Chinese specialties. The Ubin Information Kiosk, run by National Parks, is located near the jetty and has free maps and information on interesting places to visit. You have a choice of walking or renting a bicycle for a leisurely trip around the island. There are drink stalls all over the island, offering cold drinks as well as coconut milk straight from the coconut. Pulau Ubin's many fruit orchards produce delicious durian, mangosteens and rambutans in season.

Clockwise from top left: fishing on Pulau Ubin; a local bungalow on the island; cycle tours are available on the island; Kelongs (wooden houses above the water on stilts) can still be seen on Pulau Ubin

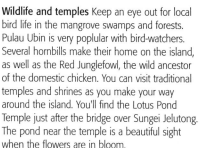

Wildlife and temples Keep an eye out for local bird life in the mangrove swamps and forests. Pulau Ubin is very poplular with bird-watchers. Several hornbills make their home on the island, as well as the Red Junglefowl, the wild ancestor of the domestic chicken. You can visit traditional temples and shrines as you make your way around the island. You'll find the Lotus Pond Temple just after the bridge over Sungei Jelutong. The pond near the temple is a beautiful sight when the flowers are in bloom.

Chek Jawa Any walk will take you by the sites of old limestone quarries, but Chek Jawa is the most visited coastal area on the island. Here you can explore the natural rocky shoreline, mangroves and beaches—look for the sand bar where you'll find starfish, crabs and sand dollars at low tide.

THE BASICS

➕ e2

🚇 MRT to Tanah Merah then bus 2 to Changi Village. It's a 10-min bumboat ride from Changi Jetty (near the Changi Village Hawker Centre) to the jetty at Pulau Ubin. Bumboats operate from sunrise to sunset

✋ Bumboat ticket inexpensive

❓ Nature walks, birdwatching and cycling tours run by the Green Volunteers Network www.gvn.com.sg. Free guided walks organized by National Parks ☎ 6542 4108, 6545 4761

More to See

DESARU

www.myoutdoor.com

Located on the eastern tip of the Malaysian peninsula, Desaru is a popular beach resort for Singaporeans, and a good introduction to Malaysian culture. Its casuarina-lined, clean, sandy white beaches are fringed by lush tropical forest. There are numerous resorts and hotels—activities include golfing, horse riding, tennis, canoeing, swimming, boating, fishing and snorkeling.

➕ Off map ✉ 78 miles (125km) northeast of Singapore. Accessible from Singapore by road via Kota Tinggi (2-hour drive), and by ferry from Changi Ferry Terminal, Mon–Thu, 3 times a day and Fri–Sun, 4 times a day ☎ 6546 8518

PULAU SEKING

As you travel to the island, you pass lots of freight ships awaiting berth in Singapore's busy harbor. The island has a small Malay settlement of brightly painted, stilt houses that stand over the sea. You may walk around the settlement and, since some villagers sell drinks, shells and coral, it's worth buying something just to get a look inside the traditional houses.

➕ b–c4 ✉ 5 miles (8km) southwest of Singapore 🚢 60-min ferry ride from Marina South Pier. Departure times: 10am and 1.30pm (Mon–Sat) and 9am, 11am, 1pm, 3pm and 5pm (Sun and public holidays) ☎ 736 8672

ST. JOHN'S ISLAND

Just 0.6 miles (km) south of the southernmost part of Sentosa, St. John's Island (formerly known as Pulau Sekijang Bendara) is a former penal settlement with idyllic, clean, sandy beaches, walking tracks and lagoons for swimming. The low-key holiday bungalows, which can accommodate 10 people, have low rents and the picnic grounds are perfect for day-trippers.

➕ c4 ✉ 4 miles (6.5km) south of Singapore 🚢 45-min ferry ride from Marina South Pier. Departure times: 10am and 1.30pm (Mon–Sat) and 9am, 11am, 1pm, 3pm and 5pm (Sun and public holidays) ☎ 736 8672

St. John's Island

Diving Singapore's Islands

Some of Singapore's offshore islands are suitable for scuba diving, although due to often strong currents, divers should take organized tours. Local dive schools conduct NAUI or PADI courses with day and night diving options.

Kusu Island

The island's two swimming lagoons are a popular destination for day-trippers. The warm fringing waters are ideal for swimming among hard and soft corals, pelagic fish, sea fans, sea snakes and turtles. Dolphins are sometimes seen. Visit the charming Chinese Temple, Da Ba Gong (Temple of the Merchant God), which attracts 130,000 people on the ninth month of lunar calendar, and the Malay shrine Kramat Kusu. And be sure to take in the stunning views of the mainland from the hilltop.

✚ Southeast of Sentosa
⛴ Ferry from Marina South Pier. Departure times: 10am and 1.30 pm (Mon to Sat), and at 9am, 11am, 1pm, 3pm and 5pm (Sun and public holidays). Return ticket S$9 adults, S$6 children 3 to 12 years. ☎ 736 8672
Average Visibility: 3ft (1m)
Maximum Depth: 100ft (30m)

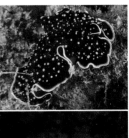

A six-banded angelfish (above) and a marine flatworm (above right)

A squid (right)

Lazarus Island and Sisters' Island

These two tiny islands, just south of Singapore, have sandy beaches and are perfect for swimming, snorkeling and scuba diving. Since the currents are strong, divers should be experienced. On the southern tip of Lazarus Island there is a wreck at 60ft (18m). Sisters' Island has a shallow reef at 20ft (6m) and a wreck at 70ft (21m).

Lazarus Island

✚ Between St. John's Island and Kusu Island

🚢 Ferry from Marina South Pier. Departure times: 10am and 1.30pm (Mon–Sat), and 9am, 11am, 1pm, 3pm and 5pm (Sun and public holidays). Return ticket S$9 adults, S$6 children 3 to 12 years. ☎ 736 8672

Average Visibility: 3ft (1m)

Maximum Depth: 60ft (18m)

Sisters' Island

✚ South of Sentosa

🚢 Ferry from Marina South Pier. Departure times: 10am and 1.30pm (Mon–Sat), and 9am, 11am, 1pm, 3pm and 5pm (Sun and public holidays). Return ticket S$9 adults, S$6 children 3 to 12 years ☎ 736 8672

Average Visibility: 5ft (1.5m)

Maximum Depth: 70ft (21m)

SURVIVING

Traveling to the islands and getting around them is hot, thirsty work and you need to understand how to prevent dehydration and how to notice if you have it. On a hot day, it may take as little as 15 minutes to become dehydrated and the following are signs: dry lips and tongue, apathy and lack of energy, muscle cramping, and bright-colored or dark urine.

To prevent dehydration
● Wear loose, light-colored clothing.
● Drink plenty of water
● Consume ample electrolytes
● Cool off by pouring some water over your head and neck.

A tigertail seahorse (above)

An icon seastar (right)

Excursions

THE BASICS

➕ Off map to southeast
🚢 Ferries leave Singapore
Cruise Centre (6270 2228)
and Tanah Merah Ferry
Terminal (6276 9722)
several times a day—the trip
takes about 45 mins.
Channel Holidays Pte Ltd
☎ 6270 2228
Auto Batam Ferries & Tours
Pte Ltd ☎ 6271 4866
Bintan Resort Ferries
☎ 6542 4369
💰 Expensive

BINTAN

Bintan Island is located about 28 miles (45km) southeast of Singapore, in the Riau Archipelago, the third largest province of Indonesia. An excellent excursion from Singapore, the island provides an introduction to Indonesian culture and, although the friendly locals speak Bahasa Indonesian, they enjoy practicing their English.

North and South Numerous seaside resorts, hotels and chalets, catering for a wide range of budgets, cover the northern shores of the island and are separated from the rest of the island by checkpoints and security guards. The southern part of the island is more populated and industrial, with electronics factories, fishing villages and bustling towns with thousands of motorcycles.

Island life Tanjung Pinang is the largest town on the island. The old, central market area, built on stilts, is a fascinating place and small enough to walk around. Try the delicious local fruit and seafood, and browse the interesting shops and markets. Pulau Penyengat, just a 10-minute bum-boat ride from Tanjung Pinang pier, has a charming fishing village, the remains of an old palace, and a mosque dating from 1880.

Practicalities Time is one hour behind Singapore time. Bring cash in rupiah for use in the local shops and street stalls; Singapore dollars and credit cards are also accepted for accommodation and food. Make sure you have your passport and check to see if you need a visa for entry. Most travelers can get a visa on arrival (VOA). Once you arrive, you fill in an arrival/departure card and pay US$10 for a 7-day stay—more for longer.

JOHOR BAHRU

Johor Bahru is located at the southern tip of the Malay Peninsula, just a short ride across the causeway from Singapore. Also referred to as JB, the state capital of Johor is a thriving commercial and administrative centre, with many shopping malls, hotels, restaurants and entertainment venues.

Choices Hotels in the city suit every taste and budget—there are resorts, international hotels and budget accommodations. Numerous nightclubs, discos, karaokes and three cinemas can be found in the heart of the city and, after sunset, a sumptuous array of food stalls appear along the streets. There are also plenty of hawker centers and restaurants offering traditional Malay, Indian and Chinese delicacies.

Shopping and Sightseeing The favourable exchange rate and tempting bargains in the big shopping malls, handicraft centers, bazaars and markets make JB is a very popular shopping destination with Singaporeans and overseas tourists. The Royal Sultan Abu Bakar Museum (Grand Palace) and its immaculate gardens, the beautiful Sultan Abu Bakar Mosque, and the Johor Art Gallery are some of JB's more famous historical and cultural attractions. The city is also a good point of departure for Malaysia's East Coast.

How to get there Take a Malaysian taxi from Rochor Road, where you can share a taxi, or book a specially licensed Singapore taxi. Buses run regularly from the Queen Street terminal in central Singapore. A ferry link operates daily between Changi Point near the Singapore International Airport and Tanjung Belungkor in Johor.

THE BASICS

➕ b1
Malaysia Tourism Promotion Board:
www.tourism.gov.my
✉ 2 Jalan Ayer Molek, Johor Bahru 80000, Johor
☎ 607 222 3590 / 3591
Fax: 607 223 5502
Taxi: Johor Taxi Service
☎ 6296 7054

Royal Sultan Abu Bakar Museum
✉ Jalan Tun Dr. Ismail, 15-min walk west of border
☎ 02 07 223 0555
🕐 Sat–Thu 9–4
💵 Expensive

Pulau Ubin Sensory Trail

Pack sunblock and water, and head to the Sensory Trail, which displays Asian plants used for food, medicines and everyday items.

DISTANCE: 1 mile (1.5km) **ALLOW:** 60–90 mins, best attempted early in the day

START

PULAU UBIN JETTY
⊞ e2 🚇 Tanah Merah, then bus 2 to Changi Village. 10-min bumboat ride from Changi Jetty to the jetty at Pulau Ubin

❶ Walk through the little village that surrounds the jetty to the Visitors' Centre, just a short distance from the jetty, on the right. Ask at the Centre for a map of the walk.

❷ The trail starts in the Spice and Herb Garden at the back of the Visitors' Centre, with a walk alongside a cool, shady banana grove. This useful plant is a good source of energy and vitamins and the leaves are used as food wrappers and disposable plates.

❸ The pathway continues past a huge field of fragrant pandan. The scented leaves are often used in Asian cooking for coloring and flavoring. Next are plantings of the grass citronella, long leafstalks of torch ginger, curry trees, climbing beans, passionfruit, guava, Aloe vera, the elephant yam, and finally a grove of sugarcane.

END

PULAU UBIN JETTY

❻ Take the trail back to the center of the main village for a look around the shops, a fresh tropical fruit drink and a delicious seafood meal. Have a rest in the shade before you head back to the mainland.

❺ Next you'll visit the island's coconut plantations, where you can take a break and buy a cold drink or try some fresh coconut milk, straight from the coconut.

❹ The trail goes on to the second section of the walk, which takes you through coastal forest and mangrove habitat. Here you'll see spiky pandanus (the leaves are used to make mats and baskets), mangrove trees, sea hibiscus (strings and cords are made from the bark), and betel nut palms (the nut is used in traditional Malay medicine).

Shopping

BINTAN MALL
You'll find a variety of clothing, specialty and gift stores, and lots of stalls selling tasty Indonesian food at this bustling mall.
➕ Off map to south
✉ Jalan Pos, Tanjung Pinang, Bintan ☎ 62 7731 8041
🕐 Daily 10–10

JOHOR BAHRU DUTY FREE COMPLEX (ZON)
The largest duty-free complex in Malaysia is packed with electronic goods, clothing and brand-name goods of all descriptions. Just 1.2 miles (2km) from the Singapore Causeway, ZON is easily accessible via daily international ferry services from Tanah Merah in Singapore.
➕ Off map to west ✉ 88 Jalan Ibrahim Sultan Stulang Laut, Johor Bahru ☎ 607221 8000 🕐 Daily 10–10
🚌 Regular buses from the Customs area from 6am–11pm

PLAZA PELANGI
A multitude of stores offer a wide array of value-for-money quality merchandise, from handicraft items and souvenirs to large selections of fashion apparel, accessories and trendy footwear. There are also eateries, a patisserie and fast-food outlets.
➕ Off map to west ✉ 2 Jalan Kuning, Taman Pelangi, Johor Bahru ☎ 607 276 2216
🕐 Daily 10–10 🚌 Regular buses from the Customs area from 6am–11pm

Restaurants

PRICES
Prices are approximate, based on a 3-course meal for one person.
$$$	over S$50
$$	S$20–S$50
$	under S$20

SEASON 'LIVE' SEAFOOD ($$)
Sit at makeshift tables under a tree, sip on fresh coconut juice and enjoy a seafood dinner of succulent steamed king prawns, tofu seafood soup, and crabs fried with spicy black pepper sauce and spring onions.
➕ 2e ✉ 59E Pulau Ubin, Singapore ☎ 6542 7627
🕐 Daily 12–2 and 5–10

TAMAN SRI TEBRAU HAWKER CENTRE ($)
Around 50 stalls sell the best Malaysian hawker fare to be found here, under one roof. Try the Penang fried kuay teow, laksa, satay, barbecued seafood or Hokkien prawn mee at prices averaging MYR3 per serving.
➕ Off map to west ✉ Jalan Keris, Johor Bahru ☎ 607 223 4935 🕐 Daily 10–10

NEW HONG KONG RESTAURANT ($)
A popular Cantonese restaurant, housed in two double-story shophouses with oriental décor, specializes in dim sum and a variety of fish, poultry and vegetable dishes, including the more expensive Chinese delicacies such as abalone and shark's fin.
➕ 1b ✉ 69–A Jalan Ibrahim Sultan, Johor Bahru ☎ 607 222 2608 🕐 Daily 12–2.30; 6–10.30

SINAR BODHI RESTAURANT ($)
Delicious and authentic Thai and Indonesian vegetarian dishes.
➕ Off map to south ✉ Jalan Bakar Batu No. 53, Tanjung Pinang, Bintan ☎ 62 771 27388 🕐 Daily 12–2 and 5–10

Where to Stay

In Singapore you'll find some of the world's best hotels, such as Raffles, while at lower prices, places such as YMCA International House offer comfortable and clean accommodation in a prime location.

Introduction 108

Budget Hotels 109

Mid-Range Hotels 110–111

Luxury Hotels 112

Introduction

Singapore is a city that caters to the whole range of accommodation styles and price ranges. Choose from backpacker hostels and boutique hotels through to top-of-the-range five-star quality hotels such as the Mandarin Oriental or historic Raffles. All are very well equiped and offer standard room facilities as well as fitness centers and spas in the more exclusive places.

For those who want to keep in touch with the business world while they are here, most hotels have international direct-dial telephones in rooms and Internet and cable access also. In many instances there are business facilities within the premises where remote meetings and conferences can take place.

Whether you want to pay a little or a lot, however, there is also the choice here between air-conditioned, 21st-century accommodation or more traditional fan-cooled rooms in areas such as Little India or Chinatown. Whatever your needs and preferences, there will be a hotel here that fits your particular bill and purse.

Be sure to make advance reservations to avoid having to compromise your budget by missing out on the low and mid-range accommodations, which are often booked out. Of course, the Internet is the way to go for bookings, and there are often seasonal specials on offer. And if you do arrive without prior reservations, the SHA counters at the airport will help you find a place to stay.

The choice of accomodation options in Singapore is excellent

STAY AT THE AIRPORT

There are many reasons—delayed flight, lost booking, convenience—why you might like to stay at Singapore's international airport. Fortunately, Terminal 2 has the Ambassador Transit Hotel, where for around S$60 per night you can rest in comfort, shower and change, swim in the pool, have a massage, or use the business center, all without the hassle of immigration and customs clearance, and without worrying about getting to the airport to catch your ongoing flight.

Budget Hotels

BEN COOLEN

www.hotelbencoolen.com
This 74-room budget hotel is near the Singapore Art Museum and Little India and not far from Orchard Road and the Marina area.
➕ F5 ✉ 47 Bencoolen Street ☎ 6336 0822 🚇 Dhoby Ghaut

BROADWAY

A Serangoon Road location puts this hotel in the middle of the Little India district. Standards are high and the staff friendly. Good Indian restaurant next door.
➕ F4 ✉ 195 Serangoon Road ☎ 6292 4661; fax 6291 6414 🚇 Bugis

LITTLE INDIA GUEST HOUSE

Facilities are basic—all rooms share a bathroom and there's no café or bar—but the location is right in the heart of Little India. Good if your budget is limited.
➕ F4 ✉ 3 Veerasamy Road ☎ 6294 2866; fax 6298 4866 🚇 Little India

LLOYD'S INN

www.lloydinn.com
Definitely budget accommodation, but all rooms are air-conditioned and have a phone and ensuite bathrooms. There are no recreational or business facilities, but there is a launderette.
➕ D5 ✉ 2 Lloyd Road ☎ 6737 7309 🚇 Somerset

METROPOLE

www.metrohotel.com
This hotel, across the street from Raffles, is a cut above basic. The famed Imperial Herbal Restaurant (▷ 92) is here.
➕ F5 ✉ 41 Seah Street ☎ 6336 3611; fax 6339 3610 🚇 City Hall

METROPOLITAN YMCA

www.mymca.org.sg
One of a number of YMCAs in Singapore, with a swimming pool. Book ahead.

➕ C3 ✉ 60 Stevens Road ☎ 6839 8333 🚇 MRT to Orchard then bus 196, 190, 132, 105, 605

NEW 7TH STOREY HOTEL

Close to Bugis MRT, this hostel/hotel offers air-conditioned rooms and dormitories.
➕ F5 ✉ 229 Rocher Road ☎ 6737 0251; fax 6334 3550 🚇 Bugis

RELC INTERNATIONAL HOTEL

www.relcih.com.sg
Excellent value and location—Orchard Road is just 10 minutes away. All rooms have a TV, a big bathroom, fridge and a balcony.
➕ C4 ✉ 30 Orange Grove Road ☎ 6885 7888 🚇 Orchard

STRAND

www.strandhotel.com.sg
A budget hotel with café and ensuite bathrooms.
➕ F5 ✉ 25 Bencoolen Street ☎ 6338 1866 🚇 Dhoby Ghaut

YMCA INTERNATIONAL HOUSE

www.mymca.org.sg
This YMCA, with a prime location near the start of Orchard Road, has a fitness facility and pool, and a McDonald's is in the building. Reserve well in advance.
➕ E5 ✉ 1 Orchard Road ☎ 6336 6000 🚇 Dhoby Ghaut

Mid-Range Hotels

PRICES

Expect to pay between S$100 and S$250 per person night for a mid-range hotel.

ALBERT COURT HOTEL
www.albertcourt.com.sg
An eight-floor hotel comprising 136 rooms in a renovated shophouse near Little India, with café and good facilities.
✚ F5 ✉ 180 Albert Street ☎ 6339 3939 🚇 Bugis

ALLSON HOTEL SINGAPORE
www.allsonhotels.com
In a good location in the Historic District, this hotel features elegant carved rosewood furniture in all of the guest rooms. Also has a small pool area and gym.
✚ F5 ✉ 101 Victoria Street ☎ 6336 0811
🚇 Bugis Junction

BERJAYA DUXTON HOTEL
www.berjayahotels-resorts.com
This classy hotel is a converted shophouse. It has one of the best French restaurants in town, which supplies excellent breakfasts (included in the room price) and dinners.
✚ E8 ✉ 83 Duxton Road ☎ 6227 7678
🚇 Tanjong Pagar

CONCORDE HOTEL SINGAPORE
www.concorde.net

A bit out of the way in Chinatown, but very reasonably priced. Outdoor pool and tennis court, two restaurants and a bar, a business area, 24-hour room service and babysitting.
✚ D7 ✉ 317 Outram Road ☎ 6733 0188 🚇 Chinatown

THE ELIZABETH SINGAPORE
www.theelizabeth.com
This small, comfortable hotel features a 3-story-high series of waterfalls. Excellent value and good location. Restaurant, small outdoor pool and fitness area, 24-hour room service and babysitting.
✚ D4 ✉ 24 Mount Elizabeth ☎ 6738 1188 🚇 Orchard

EXCELSIOR HOTEL
Very well located, with Chinatown, the colonial Civic District, Boat Quay,

LOCATION

Singapore's mid-range hotels are scattered throughout the city center, and it is worth trying to find a hotel that suits your sightseeing tastes as much as your budget. Shoppers could consider the many Orchard Road and surrounds options, while lovers of Chinese art and culture may find that staying in Chinatown provides plenty of opportunity to seek out architectural and cultural aspects of Singapore that are fast disappearing.

Clarke Quay and Marina Bay all a stone's throw away. Swimming pool.
✚ F6 ✉ 3–5 Coleman Street ☎ 6337 2200; fax 6339 3847 🚇 City Hall

FURAMA HOTEL SINGAPORE
www.furama-hotels.com
In a great location in Chinatown, near Boat Quay and Clarke Quay, where there's plenty of shopping, dining and nightlife. Outdoor pool, two restaurants, non-smoking rooms, and fitness and business facilities.
✚ E7 ✉ 60 Eu Tong Sen Street ☎ 6533 3888
🚇 Chinatown

GARDEN HOTEL
This pleasant hotel is slightly off the beaten track, but represents very good value, with the facilities of a much fancier place, including a pool. Within walking distance of Orchard and Scotts roads.
✚ C4 ✉ 14 Balmoral Road, Bukit Timah ☎ 6235 3344; fax 6235 9730 🚇 Newton

HOTEL GRAND CENTRAL
www.grandcentral.com.sg
Right in the Orchard Road area, this hotel is very popular, so make sure you book in advance. Has a restaurant, outdoor pool, fitness area, tour desk and business facilities.
✚ E5 ✉ 22 Cavenagh Road ☎ 6737 9944 🚇 Dhoby Ghaut

HOTEL WINDSOR

www.hotelwindsor.com.sg
Good value for money
and easy access to the
East Coast make this a
popular choice. The Cafe
Windsor serves continental cuisine and tasty local
fare.

🟦 K1 ✉ 401 Macpherson
Road ☎ 6343 0088
🔵 Aljunied

INN AT TEMPLE STREET

www.theinn.com.sg
Right in the heart of
Chinatown, this charming
hotel has traditional
Peranakan furniture in the
lobby and guest rooms.
Its café serves Western
and Asian dishes.

🟦 E7 ✉ 36 Temple Street,
Chinatown ☎ 6221 5333
🔵 84, 166, 197

PENINSULA EXCELSIOR

www.ytchotels.com.sg
Top value for money. An
excellent location in the
Historic District and you
can walk to Chinatown
from here. Restaurant
and bar, two outdoor
pools, babysitting, fitness
and business facilities.

🟦 F6 ✉ 5 Coleman Street
☎ 6337 2200 🔵 City Hall

PLAZA HOTEL

www.plazapacifichotels.com
Excellent leisure facilities
here–a half-size Olympic
pool and Balinese-style
spa, café and sun deck.
Also two gyms, a sauna
and a steam room.

🟦 F5 ✉ 7500A Beach Road
☎ 6298 0011 🔵 Bugis

ROYAL

www.hotelroyal.com.sg
One of Singapore's older
hotels, with spacious
rooms at very good
rates. A five-minute walk
from Novena MRT and,
in the other direction, the
famous Newton Circus
hawker center.
Swimming pool.

🟦 D3 ✉ 36 Newton Road
☎ 6426 0168; fax 6235 8668
🔵 Novena

ROYAL PEACOCK HOTEL

www.royalpeaockhotel.com
Nestled in a row of converted shophouses in
Chinatown's relatively
low-key, red-light district,
the Royal Peacock is
awash with European
furniture and deep carpets, and bed linens are

TRAVEL TO YOUR HOTEL

Besides Singapore's modern
and efficient public transportation system, taxis are
everywhere and very affordable. Another convenient
way to travel to and from
Singapore's Changi Airport is
to take a six-seater MaxiCab
shuttle service, which operates daily from 6am to midnight. The service stops at
Concorde Hotel Singapore,
Crown Prince Hotel
Singapore, Excelsior
Peninsula Hotel and Marina
Mandarin Singapore and has
a flexible routing system
between the airport and
hotels within the city.

plum and emerald green.

🟦 E7 ✉ 55 Keong Saik Road
☎ 6223 3522 🔵 Outram
Park

SWISSÔTEL MERCHANT COURT HOTEL

www.singapore-merchant-court.com
This hotel, on the
Singapore River between
Clarke Quay and
Chinatown, is always a
good choice. The extensive facilities include a
great pool, a business
center, self-service laundry facilities and a relaxing lobby bar.

🟦 E6 ✉ 20 Merchant Road
☎ 6337 2288 🔵 Clarke Quay

TRADERS HOTEL

This is near the Botanic
Gardens and Orchard
Road. Family apartments
have small kitchens and
rooms with foldaway
beds that double as
meeting rooms for business travelers.

🟦 C4 ✉ 1A Cuscaden Road
☎ 6738 2222; fax 6831 4314
🔵 Orchard

YORK HOTEL SINGAPORE

www.yorkhotel.com.sg
A small hotel with spacious rooms, just a short
walk from Orchard Road.
Restaurant, outdoor pool
and sun deck with huge
palms, 24-room service
and babysitting.

🟦 D4 ✉ 21 Mount Elizabeth
☎ 6737 0511 🔵 Orchard

WHERE TO STAY MID-RANGE HOTELS

Luxury Hotels

PRICES

Expect to pay over S$250 per person per night for a luxury hotel.

FOUR SEASONS
www.fourseasons.com/singapore
Ideally located just behind Orchard Road, with top-notch facilities, two pools, air-conditioned tennis courts and good restaurants.
✚ C4 ✉ 190 Orchard Boulevard ☎ 6734 1110 🚇 Orchard

FULLERTON
www.fullertonhotel.com
Located in the heritage GPO building, the Fullerton has lovely river views.
✚ F7 ✉ 1 Fullerton Square ☎ 6735 8388 🚇 Raffles Place

GOODWOOD PARK
www.goodwoodparkhotel.com.sg
Formerly the Teutonia Club for German expatriates, this hotel retains its charm. It is well located, close to Orchard Road, and has lovely gardens.
✚ C4 ✉ 22 Scotts Road ☎ 6737 7411 🚇 Orchard

MARINA MANDARIN
With a superb waterfront location in the Marina Bay, this 575-room luxury hotel offers the ultimate in facilities, including a host of recreation possibilities.
✚ F6 ✉ 6 Raffles Boulevard ☎ 6845 1000; fax 6845 1199 🚇 City Hall

MARRIOTT
www.marriott.com
This Singapore landmark, formerly the Dynasty, retains its original distinctive pagoda-style roof and features a roof-top pool and business and fitness facilities. Central location above Tangs store.
✚ C4 ✉ 320 Orchard Road ☎ 6735 8967 🚇 Orchard

ORIENTAL
www.mandarin-oriental.com/singapore
The 21 floor Oriental is one of three luxury hotels built on reclaimed land overlooking Marina Bay. It is conveniently close to Marina Square shopping mall—good for last-minute gifts—and Suntec City, which incorporates one of the largest conference and exhibition halls in Asia and is Singapore's newest central business district.
✚ F6 ✉ 5 Raffles Avenue, Marina Square ☎ 6339 8811 🚇 City Hall

GOING UP!
Don't miss the ride in the high-speed elevator of the Swissôtel the Stamford—the only way to get to the top of its 73 floors. A matter of seconds after leaving the ground you are deposited 741ft (226m) above street level.

RAFFLES
www.raffles.com
To relive the golden age of travel, stay at Raffles (▷ 34), Singapore's most famous hotel, first opened in 1887. All the accommodations are suites and are expensive.
✚ F5 ✉ 1 Beach Road ☎ 6337 1886 🚇 City Hall

RITZ-CARLTON MILLENIA
www.ritzcarlton.com
Ideal for business travelers and for visitors who can afford to splurge. A commanding position on Marina Bay provides fantastic views over the harbor and the new Esplanade theater complex.
✚ F6 ✉ 7 Raffles Avenue ☎ 6337 8888 🚇 City Hall

SHANGRI-LA
www.shangri-la.com
One of Singapore's finest hotels, with all the facilities you'd expect, plus magnificent gardens and a golf putting green.
✚ B3 ✉ 22 Orange Grove Road ☎ 6737 3644 🚇 Orchard

SWISSÔTEL THE STAMFORD
www.swissotel.com
Reputedly the tallest hotel in the world outside the United States, this luxury hotel has every possible amenity, including 16 restaurants, a business center, sports facilities and views.
✚ F6 ✉ 2 Stamford Road ☎ 6338 8585 🚇 City Hall

The more you plan your trip, the more you'll get out of your time in Singapore. Try to catch Chinese New Year (January/February), Singapore Food Festival (March), or the Great Singapore Sale (July).

Planning Ahead	**114–115**
Getting There	**116–117**
Getting Around	**118–119**
Essential Facts	**120–121**
Language	**122**
Timeline	**124–125**

Planning Ahead

When to Go

The best time to visit Singapore is around Chinese New Year, although you will need to book a hotel well in advance. July is sale time in Orchard Road, so shoppers take note. Otherwise, the city hums along year-round, catering to holiday and business travelers alike.

TIME

Singapore is 8 hours ahead of GMT, 13 hours ahead of New York, and 2 hours behind Sydney

AVERAGE DAILY MAXIMUM TEMPERATURES

JAN	FEB	MAR	APR	MAY	JUN	JUL	AUG	SEP	OCT	NOV	DEC
86°F	88°F	88°F	89°F	90°F	90°F	87°F	88°F	88°F	88°F	88°F	86°F
30°C	31°C	31°C	32°C	32°C	32°C	31°C	31°C	31°C	31°C	31°C	30°C

Weather Singapore's climate is tropical, with very few seasonal variations. The temperature range is steady, from a night-time low of 75°F (24°C) to a daily high of 88°F (31°C). December and January can be slightly cooler and May to August slightly hotter. Rainfall peaks between November and January, with the northeast monsoon. However, it rarely rains for long—usually an hour's torrential downpour at a time. During monsoon times, storms can be dramatic, with sheets of rain and intense thunder and lightning. Most occur early in the morning and in the afternoon. Humidity can sometimes reach nearly 100 percent, and averages 84 percent.

WHAT'S ON

January *River Raft Race*: All manner of rafts race on the Singapore River, plus bands, cheerleaders and food stalls.
Thaipusam: This Hindu festival displays dramatic feats of mind over matter.
January/February *Chinese New Year*: A two-day public holiday, with fireworks, stalls and dragon dances.
February Chingay Procession: A huge street carnival based on a Chinese folk festival. Lion dancers, acrobats, bands and floats.
March *Singapore Food Festival*.

April *Singapore International Film Festival*
June *Dragon Boat Festival*: 20 teams enter this longboat race.
Singapore Arts Festival: One of Asia's leading contemporary arts festivals.
July *Great Singapore Sale*: Orchard Road hosts this price-cutting month around July, to highlight Singapore as a major shopping destination.
August *National Day*: 9 August. This public holiday marks Singapore's independence from the British.

August/September *Festival of the Hungry Ghosts*: Fun and feasting.
September *Mooncake Festival*: A colorful spectacle named after the delicious mooncakes on sale.
October *Thimithi*: Fire-walking ceremony.
October/November *Festival of the Nine Emperor Gods*: A week of processions and street opera.
November *Deepavali*: Lamps are lit to celebrate the triumph of good over evil.
December *Christmas*: Orchard Road lights up.

Singapore Online

Not surprisingly, Singapore has been fully wired for broadband and has embraced the global digital culture.

www.visitsingapore.com

This dynamic site, written in 12 languages, has up-to-date details of events, exhibitions, holiday ideas and accommodations suggestions. For serious shoppers there is a list of errant retailers.

www.asia1.com.sg

Singapore's main media group's portal. Links to all major national print media websites, plus international and regional news.

www.singapore.tourism-asia.net

Plenty of up-to-date information on this site, with good sections on general travel, attractions, shopping and entertainment.

www.asiatravelmart.com

Asia's major online travel marketplace with various hotel and flight booking information, plus booking online.

www.nhb.gov.sg/MCC

Visitor information for the Asian Civilisations Museum, the Singapore Art Museum and a WWII museum at Bukit Chandu—comprehensive descriptions, photos and locations.

www.viator.com/singapore/

An excellent site where you can enter the dates of your visit and find out what's happening. Plenty of information on tours, attractions, prices and how to get there.

http://www.travelwithyourkids.com/destinations/?c=Singapore

This website gives a light-hearted insight into unusual things to do in Singapore that will be fun for both kids and adults.

GOOD TRAVEL SITES

www.fodors.com
A complete travel-planning site. You can research prices and weather; book air tickets, cars and rooms; ask questions (and get answers) from fellow travelers; and find links to other sites.

www.changi.airport.com.sg
Features arrival and departure details, airport facilities, and shopping and dining information in both terminals.

CYBERCAFÉS

Chills Café
🔵 F6 ✉ 01–07, 39 Stamford Road ☎ 6883 1016 🕐 Daily 9.30am–midnight 🎟 S$5 per hour

Surf@Café
🔵 D5 ✉ 218 Orchard Road ☎ 6732 4154 🕐 10–10 🎟 S$5 per hour

Cybernet Cafe
🔵 e2 ✉ Level 3, Terminal 2, Changi Airport ☎ 6546 1968 🕐 7am–11pm 🎟 S$8 per hour

Getting There

INFORMATION

For airport inquiries
☎ 6542 1122;
www.changiairport.com.sg.

CAR RENTAL

● Car rental is expensive and public transportation is very good.

● If you do decide to rent a car, remember that it is very expensive to take it into Malaysia; it's much better to rent one there. An area day license has to be bought to take a car into Singapore's central business district during the week and until mid-afternoon on Saturday.

● Display coupons in your windscreen in parking lots and designated parking places. Area day licenses and books of coupons can be purchased at newsagents and garages. Steep fines are incurred for failing to display licenses and coupons.

● Driving is on the left. A valid international or other recognized driving license is required.

● Insurance is included in rental fees.

AIRPORTS

Singapore's Changi Airport is 12 miles (20km) east of the city center. Flights take around 13 hours from Western Europe and around 20 hours from the US. The huge airport has two terminals, many lounges and hundreds of shops.

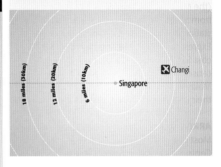

FROM CHANGI AIRPORT

Take the MRT train connection for easy access to all parts of the island. You can go to Tanah Merah station and switch to the westbound train service to be in the city in less than 30 minutes; the fare is S$1.40. Inquiries ☎ 1800 336 8900.

Taxi ranks are well marked and there is rarely a line. The fare into the city is around S$25.

The airport shuttle service (☎ 6553 3880) stops at major hotels in the city (journey time 30 minutes; cost S$7). It runs from 6am to midnight and can be picked up from just outside the terminal.

Public buses 16 and 36 travel to the city (6am to midnight, journey time 50 minutes; cost S$2). Pick them up below terminals 1 and 2.

ARRIVING BY BUS

Air-conditioned long-distance buses come direct from Bangkok, Penang and Kuala Lumpur, and from other main towns in the Malaysian peninsula. Singapore–Kuala Lumpur Express (☎ 6887 4347; www.asiatravel.com/coachtrain.com; journey time 6 hours; cost S$40). Fares to Bangkok are

S$85 for the 28-hour journey (☎ 6294 5415), with buses leaving from the Golden Mile Complex in Beach Road.

Long-distance buses from Malaysia arrive and depart from the Lavender Street bus station. Bus 170 leaves the bus station at Johor Bahru (the Malaysian city visible across the causeway from Singapore) regularly for Ban San bus station in Singapore (Singapore–Johor Bahru Express ☎ 6292 8149; journey time 1 hour; cost S$1.90). The Second Crossing, another causeway, links Tuas in Singapore's west with Malaysia's Johor state. All bus travelers break their journeys for immigration formalities.

ARRIVING BY SEA

Most cruise ships dock at the World Trade Centre. From there, taxis and buses go to central Singapore. Ferries travel regularly between Tanjong Belungkor (Johor) and Changi ferry terminal (Ferrylink ☎ 6545 3600; journey time 45 minutes; cost S$25); to and from Tioman March to October (Auto Batam Ferries ☎ 6271 4866; journey time 4 hours 30 minutes; cost S$120); and between Harbourfront and Bintan (Auto Batam Ferries ☎ 6271 4866; journey time 1 hour 30 minutes; cost S$50).

ARRIVING BY TRAIN

There is one main north–south train line in Malaysia. Around three trains arrive per day in Singapore from Kuala Lumpur. Journey times vary but average 6 hours (for KTM timetables check www.ktmb.com.my). Immigration formalities occur once you have disembarked at Singapore's Keppel Road railway station, still technically in Malaysia (☎ 6222 5165). The Eastern and Oriental Express offers a leisurely and luxurious trip to Singapore from Bangkok, Penang or Kuala Lumpur (☎ 6392 3500).

VACCINATIONS

Vaccinations are unnecessary unless you are coming from an area infected with yellow fever or cholera.

ENTRY REQUIREMENTS

Visas are not required by citizens of the EU, US or most Commonwealth countries (although Indian visitors staying more than 4 days require a visa). Passports must be valid for at least 6 months. On arrival, tourist visas are issued for 30 days. Extensions are available from the Immigration and Checkpoints Authority ☎ 6391 6100 (10 Kallang Road) www.app.ica.gov.sg or by making a trip outside Singapore. Passport and visa regulations can change at short notice, so always check before you travel.

AIRPORT HOTEL

Terminals 1 and 2 have 73 transit hotel rooms each. Rentals are from S$56 per 6-hour block for single or double occupancy.

TOURIST BOARD

● Singapore Tourism produces lots of printed material about the island's attractions and tours and there are any number of brochures available from hotel reception desks. But the Touristline is handy for after-hours information and visitor centers are always worth a visit.

Touristline: ☎ 1800 736 2000 (toll-free in Singapore). (65) 6736 2000 (overseas). Little India: ✉ 73 Dunlop Street, The InnCrowd Backpackers' Hostel, ⏰ 10–10 daily ⓡ Little India

Orchard: ✉ Junction of Cairnhill Road and Orchard Road ⏰ 9.30am to 10.30pm daily ⓡ Orchard
● Overseas tourist offices: Australia Level 11, AWA Building, 47 York Street, Sydney, NSW 2000 ☎ 02 9290 2882/8; fax 02 9290 2555
UK ✉ Carrington House, 126–30 Regent Street, London W1B 5JX ☎ 020 7437 0033; fax 020 7734 2191
US ✉ 1156 Avenue of the Americas, Suite 702, New York, NY 10036 ☎ 212/302 4861; fax 212/302 4801 and ✉ 4929 Wilshire Boulevard, Suite 510, Beverly Hills, CA 90010 ☎ 323/677 0808; fax 323 677 0801

BUSES

● Buses take exact change, though you can always give a dollar coin for a journey you know costs less.
● Buses are numerous and frequent. Buy individual tickets on the bus (exact change only), or use the ez-link card.
● Machines at the front of the bus take the card; press a button for the price of your particular journey. If you're not sure of the amount, ask the driver.
● A comprehensive bus and MRT timetable, called the Transitlink Guide, can be purchased at newsagents for S$1.50.
● Singapore Bus Service runs a hotline ⏰ Mon–Fri 8–5.30, Sat 8–1. Tell them where you are and where you want to go. The number is ☎ 1800 767 4333
● SMRT Buses also operate a night service, called the NightRider, offering late or early morning travelers a safe and affordable means of travel. The fare for this service is S$3 per trip regardless of whether you are paying by cash or ez-link card. Concessionary travel is not available for this service.

MRT

● There are three main mass rapid transit (MRT) lines; north–south, east–west and north–east.
● Trains run between 5.30am and 12.30am.
● You can buy single tickets, or use the S$7 tourist souvenir stored-value cards for a number of journeys.
● The ez-link card, also a stored-value card (minimum value S$10 plus S$5 deposit), can be used on buses as well as the MRT.
● Tickets can be purchased from machines and from ticket offices. Insert them into machines at the barriers when entering and leaving stations. Take the card with you when you are through the barrier, unless it is a single-journey ticket, in which case the machine will retain the ticket at the end of your journey.

• At the end of your stay refunds can be obtained on any amount outstanding on stored-value cards.
• Useful numbers:
• MRT ☎ 1800 767 4333; MRT and bus integration ☎ 1800 336 8900

TAXIS

• Taxis are easily found on Singapore's roads, though they can be more difficult to come by during rush hours (8am–9am and 5pm–7pm), just before midnight, and when it's raining.
• Shopping centers, hotels, sights and stations usually have taxi stands, and apart from these, taxis can also be hailed along the road. A taxi displaying a light at night is for hire.
• Taxis are air-conditioned and comfortable.
• Taxis charge a surcharge of S$2.50. There are surcharges for taxis hired from the airport, for fares between midnight and 6am, for bookings made in advance, for rush hours and for journeys via the business district or on roads where electronic road-pricing schemes are operating.
• Taxi drivers sometimes may not have sufficient change to accept large notes (S$50 or higher), so carry some low-value notes.
• Reserve in advance for important journeys, such as to the airport. Some taxi companies:
Comfort ☎ 6552 1111
Citycab ☎ 6552 2222
Comfort Premier Cabs ☎ 6552 2828

TRISHAWS

• Singapore's trishaws are now confined to a few inner-city locations where they can be hired for a ride back in time. Tour operators will also organize group tours to the back streets of Chinatown and Little India. Trishaw rides last an average of 30–45 minutes and cost from S$25 per person.
• Tour around Chinatown: Singapore Explorer ☎ 6339 6833. Trishaw tour starts from Chinatown Trishaw Park.

NEIGHBORHOODS

• Singapore's near-city neighborhoods—each one with a distinct character—are within easy reach by bus or MRT (Mass Rapid Transit). South of the river, Chinatown comes alive at festival time and just to the north is the CBD, with its tall office towers; across the river, the colonial district is set around the Padang, several museums and Raffles Hotel. Heading westward, busy Orchard Road is an international retail hub and along Serangoon Road, to the north, Indian culture thrives. Nearby Kampung Glam has long been at the heart of Malay culture. But try to discover some more out-of-the-way places, such as delightful Pulau Ubin, on the northeast of the island, or any one of the masses of public housing precincts where Singaporeans live.

VISITORS WITH DISABILITIES

Many hotels, shops and sights have facilities for people with disabilities, though getting around can sometimes be difficult because the MRT and buses are not wheelchair friendly.
If you have specific queries about particular problems, contact the National Council of Social Services ☎ 6336 1544.

Essential Facts

INSURANCE

Check your insurance policy and purchase supplementary cover if necessary. Make sure you are covered for medical expenses.

MONEY

The unit of currency is the Singapore dollar. Brunei dollar notes have the same value as the Singapore dollar and are accepted everywhere in Singapore. The Singapore dollar and other major currencies are easily changed to local currency in Malaysia and Indonesia. Traveler's checks are readily accepted.

10 dollars

50 dollars

100 dollars

1000 dollars

MAGAZINES AND NEWSPAPERS

● The main English-language dailies are the *Straits Times*, the *Business Times* and the *New Paper*. The latter is of a tabloid nature, seen as a fun alternative to others and as a result contains very little real news.

● The *International Herald Tribune* is also available, as is a wide range of local and international magazines and publications.

MAIL

● Post office hours vary, but the post office at 1 Killiney Road is open Mon–Sat 9–9, Sun 9–4.30.

● Buy stamps in small shops and hotel lobbies, as well as at post offices.

● Postcards and airmail letters to all destinations cost 50 cents. Standard letter rate to Europe/US is S$1. Prepaid postcards and airmail letters are available.

MEDICAL TREATMENT

● Singapore's medical system is world-class. It offers a mixture of public and private treatment options. Make sure you have insurance cover.

● Many hotels offer guests a doctor-on-call service or can recommend a local doctor or clinic for you.

● If you require hospital treatment, you will need to provide proof that you can pay for it.

● The best centrally located hospitals are Mount Elizabeth (☎ 6737 2666) and Gleneagles (☎ 6473 7222). Both have emergency departments.

● Most medicines are available in Singapore.

MONEY MATTERS

● You can change money at the airport on arrival, or at hotels, banks and money-changers, who can be found all over town (and whose rate is slightly better than that given by banks and hotels). Most major banks are in the Central Business District (CBD).

● ATMs are everywhere.

● Many shops, restaurants and hotels take credit cards.

OPENING HOURS
● Stores: usually Mon–Sat 10–9.30; some close earlier and others keep longer hours. Most shops are open on Sunday.
● Banks: Mon–Fri 9–3, Sat 10–12.
● Offices: usually Mon–Fri 9–5; some open for half a day on Saturday and others open earlier and close later.
● Doctors' clinics: Mon–Fri 9–6, Sat 9 to 12.

PUBLIC HOLIDAYS
● New Year's Day: 1 January
● Hari Raya Puasa: one day, January/February
● Chinese New Year: two days, January/February
● Good Friday: March/April
● Hari Raya Haji: one day, April
● Labour Day: 1 May
● Vesak Day: one day, May
● National Day: 9 August
● Diwali: November
● Christmas Day: 25 December

TELEPHONES
● Phone calls within Singapore are very cheap—local calls cost as little as 10 cents for three-minute blocks.
● Both coin- and card-operated telephones are easy to find. Most restaurants and coffee shops, as well as most shops and sights, have public phones. Phones can also be found at MRT stations.
● Phone cards can be purchased at stores and post offices.
● Calls from some hotels are subject to a 20 percent surcharge.
● International calls need to be prefixed by 001, followed by the country code. To call Singapore from outside, use country code 65.
● Operator to call for Singapore numbers ☎ 100; international numbers ☎ 104

EMBASSIES AND CONSULATES
● Australia ✉ 25 Napier Road ☎ 6836 4100 ◉ Mon–Fri 8.30–12.30 and 1.30–5
● Canada ✉ 80 Anson Road, 14–00 IBM Towers ☎ 6325 3200 ◉ Mon–Fri 8.30–11.30
● India ✉ 31 Grange Road ☎ 6737 6777 ◉ Mon–Fri 9–5.30am
● Indonesia ✉ 7 Chatsworth Road ☎ 6737 7422 ◉ Mon–Fri 8.30–5
● Ireland ✉ 541 Orchard Road, 08–00 Liat Towers ☎ 6238 7616 ◉ 9.30–12.30, 2–4.30
● Malaysia ✉ 301 Jervois Road ☎ 6235 0111 ◉ Mon–Fri 8–4.15
● New Zealand ✉ 391A Orchard Road, 15–06 Ngee Ann City Tower A ☎ 6235 9966 ◉ Mon–Fri 9.30–4
● UK ✉ 100 Tanglin Road ☎ 6424 4200 ◉ Mon–Fri 8.30–5
● US ✉ 27 Napier Road ☎ 6476 9100 ◉ Mon–Fri 8.30–3.30

LOST PROPERTY
● Police ☎ 999
● For lost credit cards: American Express ☎ 1800 737 8188;
Diners Card ☎ 6294 4222;
MasterCard ☎ 1800 110 0113;
VISA ☎ 1800 110 0344

Language

Singapore has four official languages: English, Mandarin, Malay and Tamil. English is widely understood and spoken. A patois know as Singlish is often used. Nominally English, it uses words from other languages, primarily Malay. Its clipped phrases and stresses make interesting listening. Road signs, bus destinations and tickets all appear in English, and staff in stores, hotels and places of interest speak English.

USEFUL WORDS AND PHRASES

MALAY	ENGLISH
selamat pagi	good morning
selamat petang	good afternoon
selamat malam	goodnight
selamat tinggal, selamat jalan	goodbye
api khabar?	how are you?
khabar baik	I'm fine
ya	yes
tidak	no
tidak apa	never mind
terimah kasih	thank you
sama sama	you're welcome
baiklah	OK
bila?	when?
esok	tomorrow
hari ini	today
semalam	yesterday
berapa har ganya?	how much?
mahal	expensive
murah	cheap
berapa jauh?	how far?
di mana?	where?

NUMBERS

satu	1
dua	2
tiga	3
empat	4
lima	5
sitta	6
tujuh	7
lapan	8
sembilan	9
sepuluh	10
sebelas	11
dua belas	12
tifa belas	13
dua puluh	20
tiga puluh	30
empat puluh	40
lima puluh	50
seratus	100
seribu	1,000

DAYS

senin, isnin	Monday
selasa	Tuesday
rabu	Wednesda
khamis	Thursday
jumaat	Friday
sabtu	Saturday
ahad	Sunday

FOOD AND DRINK

daging lembu	beef
ayam	chicken
ikan	fish
daging babi	pork
nasi	rice
nasi goreng	fried rice
mee goreng	fried noodles
sayur	vegetables
kopi	coffee
teh	tea

Timeline

EARLY DAYS

The first mention of Singapore comes in Chinese seafaring records of the 3rd century AD, where it is referred to as "Pu lou Chung" (island at the end of the peninsula). In the late 13th century Marco Polo noted a thriving city, possibly a satellite of the flourishing Sumatran Srivijayan empire. It could have been Singapore, then called Temasek. Sejarah Melayu (Malay annals of the 16th century) note a 13th-century Singapura (Lion City). In the late 14th century, the island's ruler, Parameswara, fled to Melaka. For 400 years Singapore was all but abandoned except for visiting pirates and fishermen.

Left to right: Sir Stamford Raffles, founder of Singapore; Raffles Hotel; plaque at Old Ford Factory; Chinatown temple detail; an old newspaper at Old Ford Factory; artwork at a Chinatown temple

1819 British official Thomas Stamford Raffles selects Singapore as a trading post between China and India. It is also near to newly acquired British colonies.

1826 With Penang and Melaka, Singapore becomes part of the British-run Straits Settlements.

1867 Singapore is designated a Crown Colony under British rule. It becomes a hub of international trade.

1870s Thousands of immigrants from south China begin arriving in Singapore. They work in shipyards and rubber plantations, and as small traders.

1887 Henry Ridley, director of the Botanic Gardens, propagates Asia's first rubber trees. Raffles Hotel opens.

1921 Japan's increasing military might causes the British to start building coastal defenses.

1942 Singapore falls to the Japanese.

1945 British Lord Louis Mountbatten accepts the Japanese surrender.

1954 Singapore's first elections: a legislative council is elected to advise the governor. Lee Kuan Yew helps found the People's Action Party (PAP).

1955 A Legislative Assembly is set up. David Marshall becomes Singapore's first chief minister.

1957 Malaya becomes independent. Singapore is a separate colony.

1959 PAP forms Singapore's first government. Lee Kuan Yew is appointed prime minister.

1963 Singapore forms the Federation of Malaysia with Malaya, Sarawak and North Borneo.

1965 Singapore leaves the Federation and becomes an independent republic.

1966 The Singapore dollar becomes the official currency.

1968 The British announce military withdrawal.

1977 2,913 acres (1,179ha) of land is reclaimed from the sea.

1990 Lee Kuan Yew steps aside, into the newly created post of senior minister.

2000 Singapore recovers from the Asian economic crisis.

2007 30th anniversary of the Singapore Arts Festival.

JAPANESE OCCUPATION

In 1942 the Japanese launched their attack on Singapore. Despite being out-numbered three to one, they gained control of the colony in just a few days, during which time tens of thousands of British, Indian and Australian troops were killed or wounded. During the occupation up to 50,000 Chinese men were executed and the Allied troops were interned or dispatched to work on the infamous "Death" railway.

LEE KUAN YEW

Lee Kuan Yew is credited with transforming Singapore from a Third World trading port to a highly developed nation. Known for hard work and discipline, he encouraged developments in housing, education, infrastructure and manufacture, with amazing results.

Index

A

accommodation 17, 107–112
air-conditioning 4, 10
airport 116
airport hotel 108, 117
amusement parks
　Haw Par Villa 70–71
　Sentosa Island 8, 17, 60–61
antiques 11, 12, 73, 90
Arab Street 38
Asian Civilizations Museum
　8, 24–25
ATMs 120

B

banks 120, 121
bars and clubs 13, 17, 18,
　44–45, 91
beaches 81
Big Splash water rides 81
Bintan Island 102
Bishan HDB Estate 86
bookshops 73
Botanic Gardens 8, 52–53
budget travel 17, 109
Bugis Street 38
Bukit Timah Nature Reserve
　18, 64, 65
buses
　long-distance 116–117
　Singapore 118

C

cableskiing 81
car rental 116
Carlsberg Sky Tower 61
carpet auctions 73
Central Sikh Temple 86
Changi Chapel and Museum
　8, 78
Chek Jawa 97
Chettiar Temple 38
children's activities 17
Chinatown 9, 17, 26–27, 119
Chinese Garden 70
the city 20–48
　entertainment and nightlife
　　44–45
　map 22–23
　restaurants 46–48
　shopping 42–43
　sights 24–40
　walk 41
City Hall 40
Clarke Quay 38–39, 42
classical music venues 28, 45
climate and seasons 114
coffee shops 74
colonial residences 70
comedy venues 44
credit cards 121
cricket 40
cruise ships 117
cybercafés 115

D

Da Ba Gong 100
dance, Indian 91
dehydration 101
department stores 10, 12, 33,
　42, 43
Desaru 98
disabilities, visitors with 119
doctors 120, 121

E

East Coast Park 9, 80–81, 88
East Coast Sailing Centre 81
east island 75–92
　entertainment and nightlife
　　91
　map 76–77
　restaurants 92
　shopping 90
　sights 78–87
　walk 88
eating out 14, 16
　coffee 14
　hands or cutlery 14
　hawker food stands 15, 16,
　　106
　popiah (pancakes) 47
　satay 46
　'steamboat' 92
　see also restaurants
electrical and electronic
　goods 10, 12, 16, 42, 43, 90
embassies and consulates
　121
entertainment and nightlife
　13, 17
　the city 44–45
　east island 91
　listings 44
Esplanade 9, 18, 28
excursions 100–103

F

fabrics 38, 90
fashion shopping 16, 42
ferries 117
festivals and events 114
fines 5
foreign exchange 120
Fuk Tak Chi Museum 27, 39

G

gardens
　Botanic Gardens 8, 52–53
　Chinese Garden 70
　Japanese Gardens 70
　Mandai Orchid Gardens 9,
　　56
　National Orchid Garden
　　53, 72
golf 81

H

Harbourfront 70
Haw Par Villa 70–71

health 117, 120
history 124–125
hong bao 42
hospitals 120
hostels 109
hotels 108, 109–112

I

insurance 120

J

jade 73
Japanese Gardens 70
jewelry and watches 12, 43,
　90
Johor Art Gallery 103
Johor Bahru 103
Joo Chiat Road 9, 79
Jurong BirdPark 9, 18, 54–55

K

Kampung Glam 9, 29, 119
Kramat Kusu 100
Kranji War Memorial 71
Kusu Island 5, 100

L

language 122
Lazarus Island 101
Little India 9, 30–31
lost property 121
Lotus Pond Temple 97

M

MacRitchie Reservoir Park
　64–65
mail 120
Malay Village 86–87
Mandai Orchid Gardens 9, 56
Marina Cove 81
Maritime Museum 61
markets 11, 31, 38, 42, 79, 87
medical treatment 120
Memories at Old Ford
　Factory 9, 57
money 120
mosques
　Nagore Durgha 39–40
　Sultan Abu Bakar Mosque
　　103
　Sultan Mosque 29
MRT (mass rapid transit) 118–
　119
museums and galleries
　Asian Civilizations Museum
　　8, 24–25
　Changi Chapel and
　　Museum 8, 78
　Fuk Tak Chi Museum 27,
　　39
　Johor Art Gallery 103
　Maritime Museum 61
　Memories at Old Ford
　　Factory 9, 57
　Museum of Shanghai Toys

39
National Musuem of
  Singapore 40
NUS Centre for the Arts 71
Raffles Museum 34
Republic of Singapore Air
  Force Musuem 8, 82–83
Royal Sultan Abu Bakar
  Museum 103
Singapore Art Museum 8,
  35
Singapore Discovery
  Centre 8, 62–63
Singapore Science Centre
  8, 17, 66–67

N
Nagore Durgha 39–40
National Musuem of
  Singapore 40
National Orchid Garden 53,
  72
nature reserves 8, 18, 64–65,
  87
neighborhoods 119
netball 91
Newater Visitor Centre 87
newspapers and magazines
  120
Ngee Ann City 33
night market 38
Night Safari 9, 18, 58–59
NUS Centre for the Arts 71

O
office hours 121
Omni Theater 63
opening hours 121
Orchard Road 9, 10, 32–33,
  119

P
Padang 40, 119
Pasir Ris Park 87
passports and visas 117
Phor Kark See 86
Planetarium 63
population 4
postal service 120
public holidays 121
public transport 118–119
Pulau Penyengat 102
Pulau Seking 98
Pulau Ubin 9, 96–97, 119
Pulau Ubin Sensory Trail 104

R
Raffles Hotel 9, 34
Raffles Museum 34
religions 4
Republic of Singapore Air
  Force Musuem 8, 82–83
restaurants 15
  the city 46–48

east island 92
Singapore environs 105
west island 74
rock climbing wall 91
Royal Sultan Abu Bakar
  Museum 103

S
sailing 81
St. John's Island 5, 98
scuba diving 100–101
Sentosa Island 8, 17, 60–61
shophouses 27
shopping 10–12, 16, 32–33
  bargaining 11, 43
  the city 42–43
  consumer protection 11
  east island 90
  Great Singapore Sale 10
  opening hours 121
  Singapore environs 106
  west island 73
shopping malls 12, 28, 33,
  42, 43, 73
Singapore Art Museum 8, 35
Singapore Discovery Centre
  8, 62–63
Singapore environs 93–106
  excursions 102–103
  map 94–95
  restaurants 106
  shopping 106
  sights 96–99
Singapore Science Centre 8,
  17, 62–63
Singapore Zoo 8, 68–69
Singlish 4
Siong Lim Temple 8, 84–85
Sisters' Island 101
Sri Mariamman Temple 8,
  36–37
Sri Srinivasa Perumal Temple
  31
Sri Veeramakaliamman
  Temple 31
Sultan Abu Bakar Mosque
  103
Sultan Mosque 29
Sungei Buloh Wetland
  Reserve 18, 65

T
Tanjung Pinang 102
taxis 119
telephones 121
temples
  Central Sikh Temple 86
  Chettiar Temple 38
  Da Ba Gong 100
  Lotus Pond Temple 97
  Phor Kark See 86
  Siong Lim Temple 8, 84–85
  Sri Mariamman Temple 8,
    36–37

Sri Srinivasa Perumal
  Temple 31
Sri Veeramakaliamman
  Temple 31
Thian Hock Keng Temple
  27
tennis 81
theater 28, 91
Theatres on the Bay 9, 28
Thian Hock Keng Temple 27
Tiger Balm Gardens 70–71
time differences 114
tourist information 115, 118
train services 117
traveler's checks 120
travelling to Singapore 116–
  117
trishaws 119
turtle sanctuary 5
two-day itinerary 6–7

V
vaccinations 117

W
walks
  the city 41
  East Coast Park 88
  National Orchid Garden 72
  Pulau Ubin Sensory Trail
    104
websites 115
west island 49–74
  map 50–51
  restaurants 74
  shopping 73
  sights 52–71
  walk 72
wildlife 18, 54–55, 58–59, 64–
  65, 87, 97

Y
YMCA 17, 109

Z
zoos
  Night Safari 9, 18, 58–59
  Singapore Zoo 8, 68–69

CITYPACK TOP 25
Singapore

WRITTEN BY Vivien Lytton
ADDITIONAL WRITING Rod Ritchie
DESIGN CONCEPT Kate Harling
ALL DESIGN WORK Jackie Bailey
INDEXER Marie Lorimer
IMAGE RETOUCHING AND REPRO Michael Moody and Sarah Butler
SERIES EDITOR Paul Mitchell

© **AUTOMOBILE ASSOCIATION DEVELOPMENTS LIMITED 2007**

First published 1996
Reprinted September 2008
Colour separation by Keenes
Printed and bound by Leo, China
A CIP catalogue record for this book is available from the British Library.

ISBN 978-0-7495-5251-0

The contents of this publication are believed correct at the time of printing.
Nevertheless, the publishers cannot be held responsible for any errors or omissions or
for changes in the details given in this guide or for the consequences of any reliance
on the information provided by the same. This does not affect your statutory rights.
Assessments of attractions, hotels, restaurants and so forth are based upon the
author's own personal experience and, therefore, descriptions given in this guide nec-
essarily contain an element of subjective opinion which may not reflect the publishers'
opinion or dictate a reader's own experiences on another occasion. We have tried to
ensure accuracy in this guide, but things do change and we would be grateful if read-
ers would advise us of any inaccuracies they may encounter.

Published by AA Publishing, a trading name of Automobile Association Developments
Limited, whose registered office is Fanum House, Basing View, Basingstoke, Hampshire
RG21 4EA. Registered number 1878835.

A03943
Maps in this title produced from:
 mapping © MAIRDUMONT / Falk Verlag 2007
 map data supplied by Global Mapping, Brackley, UK. © Global Mapping
Transport map © Communicarta Ltd, UK

The Automobile Association would like to thank the following photographers, companies and picture libraries for their assistance in the preparation of this book.

Abbreviations for the picture credits are as follows: - (t) top; (b) bottom; (l) left; (r) right; (c) centre; (AA) AA World Travel Library.

Front Cover AA/N Setchfield; Back Cover (i) Singapore Tourism Board; Back Cover (ii) AA/C Sawyer; Back Cover (iii) AA/K Paterson; Back Cover (iv) Singapore Tourism Board; 1 AA/N Setchfield; 2-18 Singapore Tourism Board; 4tl AA/N Setchfield; 5 AA/N Setchfield; 6cl AA/N Setchfield; 6c AA/N Setchfield; 6cr Singapore Tourism Board; 6bl AA/N Setchfield; 6bc Singapore Tourism Board; 6br Singapore Tourism Board; 7cl Media Bank; 7c AA/N Setchfield; 7cr Singapore Tourism Board; 7bl Singapore Tourism Board; 7br Brand X Pictures; 10tr Singapore Tourism Board; 10tcr AA/N Setchfield; 10/11c AA/N Setchfield; 10/11b AA/N Setchfield; 11tl AA/N Setchfield; 11tcl Singapore Tourism Board; 12 Singapore Tourism Board; 13 (i) Singapore Tourism Board; 13 (ii) Singapore Tourism Board; 13 (iii) AA/N Setchfield; 13 (iv) Singapore Tourism Board; 13 (v) Singapore Tourism Board; 14tr AA/N Setchfield; 14tcr AA/N Setchfield; 14cr AA/N Setchfield; 14br Singapore Tourism Board; 15b AA/N Setchfield; 16tr Singapore Tourism Board; 16cr AA/N Setchfield; 16bcr AA/N Setchfield; 16br AA/K Paterson; 17tl AA/N Setchfield; 17cl AA/A Kouprianoff; 17bcl AA/N Setchfield; 17bl AA/N Setchfield; 18tr AA/K Paterson; 18cr AA/N Setchfield; 18bcr AA/N Setchfield; 18br AA/N Setchfield; 19 (i) AA/N Setchfield; 19 (ii) Singapore Tourism Board; 19 (iii) AA/N Setchfield; 19 (iv) The Hantu Blog; 20/21 Singapore Tourism Board; 24tl AA/N Setchfield; 24tr AA/N Setchfield; 24/25c AA/N Setchfield; 25tr AA/N Setchfield; 25cl AA/N Setchfield; 25cr AA/N Setchfield; 26tl AA/N Setchfield; 26tr AA/N Setchfield; 26cr AA/N Setchfield; 27t Singapore Tourism Board; 27cr AA/N Setchfield; 27cl AA/N Setchfield; 28tl AA/N Setchfield; 28tr AA/N Setchfield; 29tl AA/N Setchfield; 29tc Singapore Tourism Board; 29tr AA/N Setchfield; 30tl AA/N Setchfield; 30/31t AA/N Setchfield; 30/31c AA/N Setchfield; 31t Singapore Tourism Board; 31cl AA/N Setchfield; 31cr AA/N Setchfield; 32tl AA/N Setchfield; 32/33t AA/N Setchfield; 32/33c AA/N Setchfield; 33t Singapore Tourism Board; 33cl AA/N Setchfield; 33cr AA/N Setchfield; 34tl AA/N Setchfield; 34tc Media Bank; 34tr AA/N Setchfield; 35tl AA/N Setchfield; 35tc AA/N Setchfield; 35tr AA/N Setchfield; 36tl AA/N Setchfield; 36tc Singapore Tourism Board; 36tr AA/N Setchfield; 37 AA/N Setchfield; 38-41 AA/N Setchfield; 38bl AA/N Setchfield; 38br AA/N Setchfield; 39bl AA/N Setchfield; 39br AA/N Setchfield; 40nl AA/N Setchfield; 40br AA/N Setchfield; 41t AA/N Setchfield; 42t AA/N Setchfield; 43t AA/N Setchfield; 44/45t Singapore Tourism Board; 46t AA/N Setchfield; 47t AA/N Setchfield; 48 AA/N Setchfield; 49 Singapore Tourism Board; 52tl AA/N Setchfield; 52/53t AA/N Setchfield; 52/53c AA/N Setchfield; 53t AA/N Setchfield; 53cl AA/N Setchfield; 53cr AA/N Setchfield; 54tl AA/N Setchfield; 54/55t Singapore Tourism Board; 54/55c AA/N Setchfield; 55t Singapore Tourism Board; 55cl AA/N Setchfield; 55cr AA/N Setchfield; 56tl AA/N Setchfield; 56tr Singapore Tourism Board; 57tl AA/N Setchfield; 57tr AA/N Setchfield; 58tl Singapore Zoo & Night Safari; 59t Singapore Zoo & Night Safari; 59cl Singapore Zoo & Night Safari; 59cr Singapore Zoo & Night Safari; 60tl AA/N Setchfield; 60/61t AA/A Kouprianoff; 60cl AA/N Setchfield; 60/61c AA/N Setchfield; 61t AA/N Setchfield; 61cl AA/N Setchfield; 61cr AA/N Setchfield; 62tl AA/N Setchfield; 62tc Singapore Discovery Centre; 62tr AA/N Setchfield; 63 AA/N Setchfield; 64tl AA/N Setchfield; 64/65c AA/N Setchfield; 66tl AA/N Setchfield; 66/67t AA/N Setchfield; 66/67c AA/N Setchfield; 67t AA/N Setchfield; 67cl AA/N Setchfield; 67cr AA/N Setchfield; 68tl Singapore Zoo & Night Safari; 68/69t Singapore Zoo & Night Safari; 68/69c Singapore Tourism Board; 69tl Singapore Tourism Board; 69tr Singapore Zoo & Night Safari; 69cl Singapore Zoo & Night Safari; 69cr Singapore Zoo & Night Safari; 70-71t AA/N Setchfield; 70bl Singapore Tourism Board; 70br AA/N Setchfield; 71bl AA/N Setchfield; 71br AA/N Setchfield; 72t AA/N Setchfield; 73t AA/N Setchfield; 74t Singapore Tourism Board; 75 AA/N Setchfield; 78tl Singapore Tourism Board; 78tr AA/N Setchfield; 79tl AA/N Setchfield; 79tr AA/N Setchfield; 80tl AA/N Setchfield; 80/81t AA/N Setchfield; 80/81c AA/N Setchfield; 81t AA/N Setchfield; 81c AA/N Setchfield; 82t AA/N Setchfield; 82cl AA/N Setchfield; 82cr AA/N Setchfield; 83t AA/N Setchfield; 83cl AA/N Setchfield; 83cr AA/N Setchfield; 84tl AA/N Setchfield; 84ct AA/N Setchfield; 84tr AA/N Setchfield; 85 AA/N Setchfield; 86-87r AA/N Setchfield; 87b AA/N Setchfield; 87bl AA/N Setchfield; 87br AA/N Setchfield; 88t AA/N Setchfield; 89 AA/N Setchfield; 90t AA/N Setchfield; 91t Singapore Tourism Board; 92t Singapore Tourism Board; 93 The Hantu Blog; 96tl AA/N Setchfield; 97/97 AA/N Setchfield; 96bl Singapore Tourism Board; 97 AA/N Setchfield; 98t AA/N Setchfield; 98b AA/N Setchfield; 99 AA/K Paterson; 100/101t The Hantu Blog; 100bl The Hantu Blog; 100cr The Hantu Blog; 100br The Hantu Blog; 101bl The Hantu Blog; 101br The Hantu Blog; 102t AA/S Strange; 102bl © Leonid Serebrennikov/Alamy; 102br © Leonid Serebrennikov/Alamy; 103t AA/N Setchfield; 103bl AA/N Hanna; 103bcr AA/N Setchfield; 103br AA/N Setchfield; 104t Singapore Tourism Board; 105t AA/N Setchfield; 105c Singapore Tourism Board; 106 AA/N Setchfield; 107 AA/N Setchfield; 108-112t AA/C Sawyer; 108tr Media Bank; 108tcr Media Bank; 108cr AA/N Ray; 108br AA/N Setchfield; 113 Singapore Tourism Board; 114-125 Singapore Tourism Board; 123 AA/N Setchfield; 124bl AA/N Setchfield; 124bc AA/N Setchfield; 124br AA/N Setchfield; 125bl AA/N Setchfield; 125bc AA/N Setchfield; 125br AA/N Setchfield

Every effort has been made to trace the copyright holders, and we apologise in advance for any accidental errors. We would be happy to apply the corrections in the following edition of this publication.